ORTHODOX DAILY PRAYERS

COLLECTOR'S EDITION

with Instructions and Index

by Anonymous
Nuns and Clergy

Orthodox Daily Prayers
Collector's Edition
with Instructions and Index
by Anonymous Nuns and Clergy

ISBN 978-1-77335-148-3

Cover Design, Book Layout, Index
by Magdalene Pagratis

Orthodox Daily Prayers
First published by
Saint Tikhon's Seminary Press in 1982

Printed with the blessings of His Grace,
the Right Reverend Herman
Bishop of Philadelphia
and Eastern Pennsylvania

This edition is published by Angel Books,
Dorval, Quebec, 2024

Contents

INTRODUCTION 4

MORNING PRAYERS 8

COMMEMORATION OF THE LIVING AND THE DEAD 25

PRAYERS AT THE TABLE 32

THE ORDER OF COMPLINE 36

BEFORE SLEEP 62

THE THREE CANONS 79

CANON IN PREPARATION FOR HOLY COMMUNION 109

PRAYERS IN PREPARATION FOR HOLY COMMUNION 119

PRAYERS OF THANKSGIVING AFTER COMMUNION 145

INDEX 153

INTRODUCTION

THE PRAYERBOOK

The present Prayerbook contains the most basic daily prayers of the Orthodox Christian as they have been transmitted to us essentially by the Russian Church, although the other Orthodox Traditions in this matter are very similar.

In this book, we will find the Psalms of the Holy Prophet King David, the prayer which Our Lord Himself taught His holy disciples, prayers of the desert fathers, prayers of the great hierarchs and teachers of the Church, as well as the prayers of more recent fathers.

The publication of such prayers does not limit the free expression of the Christian soul to the Creator, the Mostholy Theotokos and the Saints. On the contrary, by reading these prayers we learn how to pray. They become models for our own, personal prayers. Often, we would like to pray but, distracted by the bustling world around us, or troubled by fear or sorrow, we do not even know how to begin. We then begin with the Prayerbook and find that not only much of what we wanted to say is included in the prayers of the fathers, but that afterwards, we find words of our own to continue the outpouring of our soul.

There is yet another gift in the Prayerbook. As Orthodox Christians we are all members of the same Body. We express and partake of that oneness in the services of the Church, especially in the Divine Liturgy. Through the Prayerbook, this oneness is brought into our homes or any place that an Orthodox Christian reads it. Our own prayers are carried to the Throne of God on the wings of prayers that have been used by the people of God for centuries. We no longer pray alone.

THE RULE OF PRAYER

Many rules of prayer have developed in the history of the Church. At no place or time has there been a uniform rule. In 19th Century Russia, for example, the rule varied considerably from one monastery to another, though certain basic elements were found in all of them. Therefore, the term "Rule of Prayer" should never be understood as a strait jacket, regulating and limiting our communion with God.

What the Rules do teach us is the importance of regularity in our life of prayer. It is better to say a few prayers every day without fail than to say a great number of prayers on an irregular, impulsive basis. Those of us who are fortunate enough to have a spiritual father should consult him before establishing our own Rule. Those of us who do not, should begin with a modest Rule, increasing it only when it has become a regular and integral part of our lives.

THE TRANSLATION

We have attempted to use a contemporary but dignified form of the English language throughout this present translation. Wherever possible, existing translations of the Orthodox Church in America have been used. For example, the Prayers in Preparation for Holy Communion are taken from the official Divine Liturgy book (Saint Tikhon's Seminary Press, 1977) with very few changes. The Psalms, verses, troparia, and prayers not included in that edition have now been translated and included to complete the traditional order.

The Psalms are taken from the Revised Standard Version of the Bible with changes made wherever significant differences with the Orthodox liturgical Psalter (based on

INTRODUCTION

the Septuagint) made it necessary. The numbering of the Psalms follows the Septuagint throughout the Prayerbook. We are leaving to Biblical scholars the study of the merits of the various texts of the Holy Scriptures. Our object here is to provide the English-speaking Orthodox Christian with a Prayerbook as closely equivalent as possible to the Prayerbooks that Orthodox Christians of other nationalities have used for generations.

MORNING PRAYERS

Having awakened, arise from your bed without laziness and, having gathered your thoughts, make the Sign of the Cross, saying:

In the name of the Father, and of the Son, and of the Holy Spirit. Amen.

Afterwards, stand in silence for a few moments until all your senses are calmed. At that point, make three prostrations, saying:

Lord Jesus Christ, Son of God, have mercy on me, a sinner.

Then, begin the Morning Prayers with these words:

Lord Jesus Christ, Son of God, through the prayers of Thy most pure Mother and all the saints, have mercy on us. Amen.

Glory to Thee, our God, glory to Thee.

O Heavenly King, the Comforter, the Spirit of Truth Who art everywhere and fillest all things. Treasury of Blessings and Giver of Life: Come and abide in us, and cleanse us from every impurity, and save our souls, O Good One.

Holy God! Holy Mighty! Holy Immortal! Have mercy on us. *(Repeat three times.)*

Glory to the Father, and to the Son, and to the Holy Spirit, now and ever and unto ages of ages. Amen.

O Most Holy Trinity! Have mercy on us! Lord, cleanse us from our sins! Master, pardon our transgressions! Holy One, visit and heal our infirmities for Thy name's sake.

Lord, have mercy! *(Repeat three times.)*

Glory to the Father, and to the Son, and to the Holy Spirit, now and ever and unto ages of ages. Amen.

Our Father, Who art in heaven, hallowed be Thy Name. Thy Kingdom come. Thy will be done, on earth as it is in heaven. Give us this day our daily bread; and forgive us our trespasses, as we forgive those who trespass against us; and lead us not into temptation, but deliver us from evil.

If there is a priest, he adds the usual exclamation.

Having arisen from sleep, we fall down before Thee, O Blessed One, and sing to Thee, O Mighty One, the angelic hymn: Holy! Holy! Holy! art Thou, O God; through the Theotokos, have mercy on us.

Glory to the Father, and to the Son, and to the Holy Spirit:

Having raised me from my bed and from sleep, O Lord, enlighten my mind and heart, and open my lips that I may praise Thee, O Holy Trinity: Holy! Holy! Holy! art Thou, O God; through the Theotokos, have mercy on us.

Now and ever and unto ages of ages. Amen.

The Judge will come suddenly and the acts of every man will be revealed; but in the middle of the night we cry with fear: Holy! Holy! Holy! art Thou, O God; through the Theotokos, have mercy on us.

Lord, have mercy! *(Repeat twelve times.)*

Having risen from sleep, I thank Thee, the Holy Trinity. In the abundance of Thy kindness and long patience, Thou hast not been angry with me for my laziness and sinfulness, nor hast Thou destroyed me in my lawlessness. Instead, in Thy usual love for mankind, Thou hast raised me as I lay in despair, that I might rise early and glorify Thy Reign. Enlighten now the eyes of my mind and open my lips, that I might learn of Thy words, understand Thy commandments, accomplish Thy will, hymn Thee in heart-felt confession and praise Thine all-holy name, the

Father and the Son, and the Holy Spirit, now and ever and unto ages of ages. Amen.

Come, let us worship God, our King!

Come, let us worship and fall down before Christ, our King and our God!

Come, let us worship and fall down before Christ Himself, our King and our God!

Psalm 50

Have mercy on me, O God,
>   according to Thy great mercy;
> according to the multitude of Thy tender mercies,
>   blot out my transgressions.
> Wash me thoroughly from my iniquity,
>   and cleanse me from my sin!
> For I know my transgressions,
>   and my sin is ever before me.
> Against Thee, Thee only, have I sinned,
>   and done that which is evil in Thy sight,
> so that Thou art justified in Thy sentence
>   and blameless in Thy judgment.
> Behold, I was brought forth in iniquity,
>   and in sins did my mother conceive me.

Behold, Thou desirest truth in the inward being;
>therefore teach me wisdom in my secret heart.

Purge me with hyssop, and I shall be clean;
>wash me, and I shall be whiter than snow.

Fill me with joy and gladness;
>let the bones which Thou hast broken rejoice.

Hide Thy face from my sins,
>and blot out all my iniquities.

Create in me a clean heart, O God,
>and put a new and right spirit within me.

Cast me not away from Thy presence,
>and take not Thy Holy Spirit from me.

Restore to me the joy of Thy salvation,
>and uphold me with a willing spirit.

Then I will teach transgressors Thy ways,
>and sinners will return to Thee.

Deliver me from bloodguiltiness, O God,
>Thou God of my salvation,
>and my tongue will sing aloud of Thy deliverance.

O Lord, open Thou my lips,
>and my mouth shall show forth Thy praise.

For Thou hast no delight in sacrifice;
>were I to give a burnt offering, Thou wouldst not be pleased.

The sacrifice acceptable to God is a broken spirit;
>a broken and contrite heart, O God, Thou wilt not despise.

Do good to Zion in Thy good pleasure;
>rebuild the walls of Jerusalem,

Then wilt Thou delight in right sacrifices,
>in burnt offerings and whole burnt offerings; then bulls will be offered on Thy altar.

The Symbol of Faith

I believe in one God, the Father Almighty, Maker of Heaven and Earth, and of all things visible and invisible.

And in one Lord Jesus Christ, the Son of God, the only-begotten, begotten of the Father before all ages. Light of Light; true God of true God; begotten, not made; of one essence with the Father, by Whom all things were made; who for us men and for our salvation came down from Heaven, and was incarnate of the Holy Spirit and the Virgin Mary, and became man. And He was crucified for us under Pontius Pilate, and suffered, and was buried. And the third day He arose again, according to the Scriptures, and ascended into Heaven, and sits at the right hand of the Father; and He shall come again with glory to judge the living and the dead; whose Kingdom shall have no end.

And in the Holy Spirit, the Lord, the Giver of Life, Who proceeds from the Father; Who with the Father and the Son together is worshipped and glorified; Who spoke by the prophets. In one Holy, Catholic, and Apostolic Church. I acknowledge one baptism for the remission of sins. I look for the resurrection of the dead, and the life of the world to come. Amen.

1st Prayer, by Saint Macarius the Great

O God, cleanse me a sinner, for I have done nothing good before Thee. Deliver me from the evil one, and may Thy will be in me, that I might open my unworthy lips without condemnation and praise Thy holy name, Father, Son, and Holy Spirit, now and ever and unto ages of ages. Amen.

2nd Prayer, by Saint Macarius the Great

Having risen from sleep, I offer Thee, O Savior, the midnight song. Falling down, I cry to Thee: let me not fall asleep in the death of sin. Be gracious to me, Thou Who wast willingly crucified. Raise me quickly as I lie in laziness, and save me as I stand in prayer. After the night's sleep, O Christ God, shine a sinless day on me and save me.

3rd Prayer, by Saint Macarius the Great

Having risen from sleep, I run to Thee, O Master, for Thou lovest mankind, and I rush to accomplish Thy work. Help me, I pray Thee, at all times and in all things. Deliver me from every evil thing of this world and from works of the devil. Save me, and lead me into Thine eternal Kingdom. Thou art my Maker, The Provider and Giver of everything good. All my hope is in Thee and I glorify Thee, now and ever and unto ages of ages. Amen.

4th Prayer, by Saint Macarius the Great

O Lord, through Thy abundant goodness and great generosity, Thou hast allowed me, Thy servant, to pass through the hours of this night untempted by any evil of the enemy. Grant also, O Master and Creator of all, that I might accomplish Thy will in Thy true light and with an illumined heart, now and ever and unto ages of ages. Amen.

5th Prayer, by Saint Macarius the Great

O Lord, the Almighty God, Who acceptest the thrice-holy hymn from Thy heavenly hosts: accept this song of the night even from me, Thine unworthy servant. Grant that at every year and hour of my life I might glorify Thee, the Father, the Son and the Holy Spirit, now and ever and unto ages of ages. Amen.

6th Prayer, by Saint Basil the Great

Almighty Lord, the God of hosts and of all flesh, Thou livest in the heights, yet lookest down on the humble, proving the hearts and emotions, clearly foreknowing the secrets of men. Thou art the Light without beginning, in Whom there is no variation nor shadow of change. O Immortal King, accept the prayers which we now offer Thee from defiled lips. Free us from the sins we have committed in deed, word or thought, knowingly and unknowingly. Cleanse us from all defilement of flesh and spirit. Grant us to pass through the entire night of this present life with a watchful heart and a sober mind, awaiting the coming of the bright and manifest day of Thine only-begotten Son, our Lord, God and Savior Jesus Christ, when the Judge of all will come with glory to reward each according to his deeds. May we not be found fallen and lazy, but alert and roused to action, prepared to enter into His joy and the divine chamber of His glory, where the voice of those who feast is unceasing and indescribable is the delight of those who behold the inexpressible beauty of Thy countenance. For Thou art the true Light which enlightens and sanctifies all, and all creation hymns Thee unto ages of ages. Amen.

7th Prayer, also by Saint Basil

We bless Thee, most high God and Lord of mercies, Who ever doest great and unfathomable things for us— glorious and awesome things without number. Thou givest us sleep for the repose of our frailty, relieving the labors of our over-burdened flesh. We thank Thee for not destroying us in our lawlessness. Instead, Thou hast shown Thy usual love for mankind, and raised us, as we lay in despair, to glorify Thy Reign. Therefore, we implore Thy boundless goodness: enlighten our thoughts and eyes, and awaken our minds from the heavy sleep of laziness. Open our lips and fill them with Thy praise, that we may unwaveringly hymn and confess Thee, the God glorified in all and by all, Father without beginning, with Thine only-begotten Son and Thine all-holy, and life-giving Spirit, now and ever and unto ages of ages. Amen.

8th Prayer. A Midnight Song to the Most Holy Theotokos

I hymn your Grace, O Lady,
>and pray that you grace my mind.

Teach me to walk correctly
>on the path of Christ's commandments.

Strengthen me to watch in song,
>dispelling the despair of sleep.

I am bound by fetters of sin,
>free me by your prayers, O Bride of God!

Keep me in the night and in the day,
>delivering me from warring enemies.

As you bore the life-giving God,
>give life to me, who am wounded by passions.

As you bore the unsetting Light,
>enlighten my blinded soul.

O wondrous palace of the Master,
>make me a home of the divine Spirit.

As you bore the Physician,
>heal my soul of its passion-filled years.

I am tossed in the tempest of life:
>direct me to the path of repentance.

Deliver me from the eternal flame,
>from the evil worm, and from hell.

Make me not a joy for demons,
>though I am guilty of many sins.

Make me new, most undefiled one,
> for I am aged by senseless sins.

Estrange me from all torments,
> and pray for me to the Master of all.

Grant that, with all the saints,
> I may inherit the joys of heaven.

Hear, most holy Virgin,
> the voice of your useless servant.

Grant me a torrent of tears, most pure one,
> to wash the filth of my soul.

The groans of my heart I bring you unceasingly:
> open your heart, O Lady!

Accept my prayerful service,
> and take it to the compassionate God.

You who are far higher than the angels,
> raise me above this world's confusion.

O light-bearing heavenly cloud,
> direct spiritual grace into me.

I raise in praise, all-undefiled one,
> hands and lips defiled by sin.

Deliver me from soul-corrupting harm,
> praying fervently to Christ,

To Whom glory and worship are due,
> now and ever and unto ages of ages. Amen.

9th Prayer, to Our Lord Jesus Christ

My most merciful and all-merciful God, O Lord Jesus Christ! In Thy great love, Thou didst come down and become flesh in order to save all. Again, I pray Thee, save me by Grace! If Thou shouldst save me because of my deeds, it would not be a gift, but merely a duty. Truly, Thou aboundest in graciousness and art inexpressibly merciful! Thou hast said, O my Christ: "He who believes in me shall live and never see death". If faith in Thee saves the desperate, behold: I believe! Save me, for Thou art my God and my Maker. May my faith replace my deeds, O my God, for Thou wilt find no deeds to justify me. May my faith be sufficient for all. May it answer for me; may it justify me; may it make me a partaker of Thine eternal glory; and may Satan not seize me, O Word, and boast that He has torn me from Thy hand and fold. O Christ my Savior: save me whether I want it or not! Come quickly, hurry, for I perish! Thou art my God from my mother's womb. Grant, O Lord, that I may now love Thee as once I loved sin, and that I may labor for Thee without laziness as once I labored for Satan the deceiver. Even more, I will labor for Thee, my Lord and God Jesus Christ, all the days of my life, now and ever and unto ages of ages. Amen.

10th Prayer, to the Angel, the guardian of human life

O Holy Angel, who stand by my wretched soul and my passionate life: do not abandon me, a sinner, neither depart from me because of my lack of self-control. Leave no room for the evil demon to gain control of me through the violence of this mortal body. Strengthen my weak and feeble hand, and instruct me in the path of salvation. O holy Angel of God, the guardian and protector of my wretched soul and body: forgive all the sorrows I have caused you, every day of my life. If I have sinned in this past night, protect me during this day. Keep me from every adverse temptation, that I may not anger God by any sin. Pray to the Lord for me, that He may establish me in His fear and make me, His servant, worthy of His goodness. Amen.

11th Prayer, to the Most Holy Theotokos

O Most Holy Theotokos, my Lady: through your holy and all-powerful prayers, turn away from me, your humble and unworthy servant, despair, forgetfulness, unreasonableness, indifference, and all unclean, evil and blasphemous thoughts from my wretched heart and darkened mind. Extinguish the flame of my passions, for I am poor and wretched. Deliver me from my numerous and wicked memories and fantasies. Free me from all evil acts, for you are blessed by all generations, and your most honorable name is glorified unto ages of ages. Amen.

Rejoice, O Virgin Theotokos! Mary full of Grace, the Lord is with you. Blessed are you among women and blessed is the fruit of your womb, for you have borne the Savior of our souls!

Most glorious Ever-Virgin Mother of Christ our God, bear our prayer to your Son and our God, that through you He may save our souls.

O heavenly hosts of holy Angels and Archangels, pray for us sinners.

O glorious Apostles, Prophets, Martyrs, and all Saints, pray for us sinners.

Pray to God for me holy _____ (your Patron Saint), for with fervor I run to you, swift helper and intercessor for my soul!

O Lord, save Thy people, and bless Thine inheritance. Grant victories to the Orthodox Christians over their adversaries; and by virtue of Thy Cross, preserve Thy habitation.

It is truly meet to bless you, O Theotokos, ever-blessed and most pure, and the Mother of our God. More honorable than the Cherubim, and more glorious beyond compare than the Seraphim: without defilement you gave birth to God the Word: true Theotokos, we magnify you.

Glory to the Father, and to the Son, and to the Holy Spirit, now and ever and to ages of ages. Amen.

Lord, have mercy! *(Repeat three times.)*

Lord Jesus Christ Son of God, for the sake of Thy most pure Mother, our venerable and God-bearing fathers, and all the saints, save me, a sinner. Amen.

Certain pious Christians use the following "Morning Prayer of the Last Elders of Optina" with their morning prayers.

O Lord, grant that I may meet all that this coming day brings to me with spiritual tranquility. Grant that I may fully surrender myself to Thy holy Will.

At every hour of this day, direct and support me in all things. Whatsoever news may reach me in the course of the day, teach me to accept it with a calm soul and the firm conviction that all is subject to Thy holy Will.

Direct my thoughts and feelings in all my words and actions. In all unexpected occurrences, do not let me forget that all is sent down from Thee.

Grant that I may deal straightforwardly and wisely with every member of my family, neither embarrassing nor saddening anyone.

O Lord, grant me the strength to endure the fatigue of the coming day and all the events that take place during it. Direct my will and teach me to pray, to believe, to hope, to be patient, to forgive, and to love. Amen.

COMMEMORATION OF THE LIVING AND THE DEAD

To be read daily by every monastic and pious Christian at the end of his rule of prayer.

Remember, O Lord Jesus Christ our God, Thine eternal mercies and compassion, for whose sake Thou didst become man and willingly endured crucifixion and death for the salvation of those who rightly believe in Thee. Thou didst rise from the dead and ascend into Heaven and sittest at the right hand of God the Father, looking down on the humble petitions of those who call upon Thee with their whole heart. Bow down Thine ear and hear the prayer which I, Thy useless servant, offer Thee for all Thy people as a spiritual fragrance. First of all, remember Thy Holy, Catholic, and Apostolic Church which Thou didst obtain through Thy precious Blood. Establish, strengthen, broaden, and multiply her. Give her peace and keep her eternally unassailable by the gates of hell. Calm the quarrels of the churches, put out the arrogance of the heathen, and swiftly destroy and uproot the rebellions of heresies, turning them into nothing through the power of Thy Holy Spirit.

Prostration

Save, Lord, and have mercy on the Holy Orthodox Patriarchs, our Lord, the Most Blessed _____, Archbishop of Washington, Metropolitan of All America and Canada; on our Lord, the Right Reverend _____, Bishop of _____; on priests, deacons and all the clergy whom Thou hast installed to tend Thy reason endowed flock. Through their prayers, save me also, a sinner, and have mercy on me.

Prostration

Save, Lord, and have mercy on the President of our country, on all our civil authorities and armed forces. Surround them with peace, and speak peace and goodness into their hearts for Thy Holy Church and all Thy people. In their calm may we live a calm and silent life in the True Faith and in all piety and purity.

Prostration

Save, Lord, and have mercy on our father (the name and title of the abbot of your monastery or of your parish priest) with all our brethren in Christ, and have mercy on me, who am wretched, through their prayers.

Prostration

Save, Lord, and have mercy on my spiritual father _____, and forgive my transgressions through his holy prayers.

Prostration (In Monasteries)

Save, Lord, and have mercy on all our brethren who labor in this holy community—the laborers, the lay workers, and those who work the land for this monastery, and all Christians.

(In Parishes)

Save, Lord, and have mercy on all our brethren who serve this holy Church—the parish council, the choir, the teachers, the custodians and cleaners, and all who work for our parish, and all Christians.

Prostration

(Any inapplicable terms in the following petition are simply omitted.)

Save, Lord, and have mercy on my parents _____ (if they are still living), my wife/husband _____, my children _____, my brothers and sisters and all my relatives according to the flesh, those who are close to my family, and my friends. Grant them Thy worldly and heavenly good things.

Prostration

Save, Lord, and have mercy on our fathers, brothers, and sisters who live with patient faith in the monasteries of the Holy Mountain, Russia, America, and any other place. Through their prayers, have mercy on me a sinner.

Prostration

Save, Lord, and have mercy, according to the multitude of Thy compassions, on all hieromonks, monks, and nuns, and on all who in virginity, reverence, and fasting live in monasteries, in deserts and caves, on mountains and pillars, in hermitages and cleft rocks, on islands in the sea, and who live in the True Faith in every place of Thy dominion, serving Thee piously and praying to Thee. Lighten their burden and console them in sorrow. Grant them strength and resolution in their struggles, and grant me remission of sins through their prayers.

COMMEMORATION OF THE LIVING AND THE DEAD

Prostration

Save, Lord, and have mercy on the old and the young, the poor, the orphans and widows, and on those who are in sickness and in sadness, in misfortunes and in sorrow, in war and in captivity, in prison and in exile— especially those who, being Thy servants, are persecuted for Thy sake and the Orthodox Faith by godless heathens, apostates, and heretics. Remember, visit, strengthen, and comfort them, giving them early release, freedom, and deliverance by Thy might.

Prostration

Save, Lord, and have mercy on our benefactors who have mercy on us and feed us, giving us alms and security, and ask us to pray for them, despite our unworthiness. Be Thou merciful to them and grant their every petition for salvation and the reward of eternal good things.

Prostration

Save, Lord, and have mercy on all our fathers, brothers, and sisters and all Orthodox Christians who are travelling in Thy service.

Prostration

Save, Lord, and have mercy on those whom I have caused to stumble, turning them away from the path of salvation and leading them to evil and unseemly deeds. Return them to the path of salvation by Thy Divine Providence.

Prostration

Save, Lord, and have mercy on those who hate and offend me, and do me harm. Do not let them perish because of me, a sinner.

Prostration

Enlighten with the light of Thy knowledge those who have left the Orthodox Faith and have been blinded by devastating heresies, reuniting them to Thy Holy, Catholic, and Apostolic Church.

Prostration

For the Departed

Remember, Lord, all Orthodox Patriarchs and Metropolitans; archbishops and bishops; priests and those who serve in holy orders; those who serve Thee in monastic ranks and the blessed founder of our holy community (or

Church). Grant them rest with the saints in Thine eternal dwellings.

Prostration

Remember, Lord, the souls of Thy departed servants, my parents _____ (if they are already dead), and all my relatives according to the flesh. Forgive all their sins, both voluntary and involuntary. Grant them participation in Thine eternal good things and the enjoyment of the eternal and blessed life.

Prostration

Remember, Lord, all our departed fathers, brothers, and sisters, the Orthodox Christians who lie here and everywhere in the hope of the Resurrection and eternal life. Grant them to live with Thy saints under the Light of Thy countenance. Have mercy on us also, for Thou art good and lovest mankind. Amen.

Prostration

The following is repeated three times, each with a prostration.

Grant remission of sins, Lord, to all our fathers, brothers, and sisters who have departed before us in faith and the hope of the Resurrection, and make their memory eternal.

PRAYERS AT THE TABLE

Before Breakfast

O Most Holy Trinity, have mercy on us! Lord, cleanse us from our sins! Master, pardon our transgressions! Holy One, visit and heal our infirmities for Thy name's sake.

Glory to the Father, and to the Son, and to the Holy Spirit, now and ever and unto ages of ages. Amen.

Lord, have mercy! *(Repeat three times.)*

O Christ God, bless the food and drink of Thy servants, for Thou art holy, always, now and ever and unto ages of ages. Amen.

After Breakfast

More honorable than the Cherubim, and more glorious beyond compare than the Seraphim: without defilement you gave birth to God the Word: true Theotokos, we magnify you.

Glory to the Father, and to the Son, and to the Holy Spirit, now and ever and unto ages of ages. Amen.

Lord, have mercy! *(Repeat three times.)*

God is with us, through His Grace and love for mankind, always now and ever, and unto ages of ages. Amen.

Before Lunch

Our Father, Who art in heaven, hallowed be Thy Name. Thy Kingdom come. Thy will be done, on earth as it is in heaven. Give us this day our daily bread; and forgive us our trespasses, as we forgive those who trespass against us; and lead us not into temptation, but deliver us from evil.

Glory to the Father, and to the Son, and to the Holy Spirit, now and ever and unto ages of ages. Amen.

Lord, have mercy! *(Repeat three times.)*

O Christ God, bless the food and drink of Thy servants, for Thou art holy, always, now and ever and unto ages of ages. Amen.

After Lunch

We thank Thee, Christ our God, for Thou hast satisfied us with Thine earthly gifts. Deprive us not of Thy

Heavenly Kingdom, but as Thou camest among Thy disciples, O Savior, giving them peace, so come to us and save us!

Glory to the Father, and to the Son, and to the Holy Spirit, now and ever and unto ages of ages. Amen.

Lord, have mercy! *(Repeat three times.)*

Blessed is God, Who has had mercy on us and fed us from His rich gifts, through His Grace and love for mankind, always, now and ever and unto ages of ages. Amen.

Before Supper

The poor shall eat and be satisfied, and those who seek the Lord shall praise Him; their hearts shall live forever!

Glory to the Father, and to the Son, and to the Holy Spirit, now and ever and unto ages of ages. Amen.

Lord, have mercy! *(Repeat three times.)*

O Christ God, bless the food and drink of Thy servants, for Thou art Holy, always, now and ever and unto ages of ages. Amen.

After Supper

Glory to the Father, and to the Son, and to the Holy Spirit, now and ever and unto ages of ages. Amen.

Your womb became a Heavenly Table, bearing the Heavenly Bread—Christ our God. Whoever eats of him shall not die, O Birth-giver of God, according to the word of the Nourisher of all.

More honorable than the Cherubim, and more glorious beyond compare than the Seraphim: without defilement you gave birth to God the Word: true Theotokos, we magnify you!

Thou, O Lord, hast made us glad by Thy works; in the works of Thy hands shall we rejoice. Lift up the Light of Thy countenance upon us, O Lord! Thou hast put joy in my heart. With the fruit of wheat, wine and oil have we been satisfied. In peace I will both lie down and sleep; for Thou alone, O Lord, makest me to dwell in hope.

Glory to the Father, and to the Son, and to the Holy Spirit, now and ever and unto ages of ages. Amen.

Lord, have mercy! *(Repeat three times.)*

God is with us through His Grace and love for mankind, always, now and ever and unto ages of ages. Amen.

THE ORDER OF COMPLINE

The priest gives the blessing:

Blessed is our God, always, now and ever, and unto ages of ages!

NOTE: In the absence of a priest, laymen begin with:

Through the prayers of our holy fathers, Lord Jesus Christ our God, have mercy on us!

The reader continues:

Amen! Glory to Thee, our God, glory to Thee!

O Heavenly King, the Comforter, the Spirit of Truth, who art everywhere and fillest all things. Treasury of Blessings, and Giver of Life: Come and abide in us, and cleanse us from every impurity, and save our souls, O Good One.

Holy God! Holy Mighty! Holy Immortal! Have mercy on us! *(Repeat three times.)*

Glory to the Father, and to the Son, and to the Holy Spirit, now and ever, and unto ages of ages. Amen.

O Most Holy Trinity have mercy on us. Lord, cleanse us from our sins. Master, pardon our transgressions. Holy One, visit and heal our infirmities, for Thy name's sake.

Lord, have mercy! *(Repeat three times.)*

Glory to the Father, and to the Son, and to the Holy Spirit, now and ever, and unto ages of ages. Amen.

Our Father Who art in Heaven, hallowed be Thy name. Thy Kingdom come. Thy will be done, on earth as it is in Heaven. Give us this day our daily bread; and forgive us our trespasses, as we forgive those who trespass against us; and lead us not into temptation, but deliver us from evil.

The priest exclaims:

For Thine is the Kingdom, and the power, and the glory, of the Father, and of the Son, and of the Holy Spirit, now and ever and unto ages of ages.

The reader continues:

Amen! Lord, have mercy! *(Repeat twelve times.)*

Glory to the Father, and to the Son, and to the Holy Spirit, now and ever, and unto ages of ages. Amen.

Come, let us worship God, our King!

Come, let us worship and fall down before Christ, our King and our God!

Come, let us worship and fall down before Christ Himself, our King and our God!

Psalm 50

Have mercy on me, O God,
>   according to Thy great mercy;
> according to the multitude of Thy tender mercies,
>   blot out my transgressions.
> Wash me thoroughly from my iniquity,
>   and cleanse me from my sin!
> For I know my transgressions,
>   and my sin is ever before me.
> Against Thee, Thee only, have I sinned,
>   and done that which is evil in Thy sight,
> so that Thou art justified in Thy sentence
>   and blameless in Thy judgment.
> Behold, I was brought forth in iniquity,
>   and in sins did my mother conceive me.
> Behold, Thou desirest truth in the inward being;
>   therefore teach me wisdom in my secret heart.
> Purge me with hyssop, and I shall be clean;
>   wash me, and I shall be whiter than snow.

Fill me with joy and gladness;
> let the bones which Thou hast broken
> > rejoice.

Hide Thy face from my sins,
> and blot out all my iniquities.

Create in me a clean heart, O God,
> and put a new and right spirit within me.

Cast me not away from Thy presence,
> and take not Thy Holy Spirit from me.

Restore to me the joy of Thy salvation,
> and uphold me with a willing spirit.

Then I will teach transgressors Thy ways,
> and sinners will return to Thee.

Deliver me from bloodguiltiness, O God,
> Thou God of my salvation,
> and my tongue will sing aloud of Thy
> > deliverance.

O Lord, open Thou my lips,
> and my mouth shall show forth Thy praise.

For Thou hast no delight in sacrifice;
> were I to give a burnt offering, Thou
> > wouldst not be pleased.

The sacrifice acceptable to God is a broken spirit;
> a broken and contrite heart, O God,
> Thou wilt not despise.

Do good to Zion in Thy good pleasure;
> rebuild the walls of Jerusalem,

Then wilt Thou delight in right sacrifices,
>in burnt offerings and whole burnt offerings;
>then bulls will be offered on Thy altar.

Psalm 69

O God, attend to helping me!
>O Lord, make haste to help me!

Let them be put to shame and confusion
>who seek my life!

Let them be turned back and brought to dishonor
>who desire my hurt!

Let them be turned back in their shame
>who jeer saying: "Well done! Well done!"

May all who seek Thee
>rejoice and be glad in Thee!

May those who love Thy salvation
>say evermore, "God is great!"

But I am poor and needy;
>hasten to me, O God!

Thou art my help and my deliverer;
>O Lord, do not tarry!

Psalm 142

Hear my prayer, O Lord;
> give ear to my supplications!

In Thy faithfulness answer me,
> in Thy righteousness!

Enter not into judgment with Thy servant;
> for no man living is righteous before Thee.

For the enemy has pursued my soul;
> he has crushed my life to the ground;
>> he has made me sit in darkness like those long dead.

Therefore my spirit faints within me;
> my heart within me is appalled.

I remember the days of old,
> I meditate on all Thou hast done;
> I muse on what Thy hands have wrought.

I stretch out my hands to Thee;
> my soul thirsts for Thee like a parched land.

Make haste to answer me, O Lord!
> My spirit fails!

Hide not Thy face from me,
> lest I be like those who go down to the Pit.

Let me hear in the morning of Thy steadfast love,
> for in Thee I put my trust

Teach me the way I should go,

for to Thee I lift up my soul.
Deliver me, O Lord, from my enemies!
    I have fled to Thee for refuge!
Teach me to do Thy will,
    for Thou art my God!
Let Thy Good Spirit lead me
    on a level path!
For Thy name's sake, O Lord, give me life!
    in Thy righteousness bring my soul out of trouble!
And in Thy steadfast love cut off my enemies
    and destroy all those who afflict my soul,
    for I am Thy servant.

The Doxology

Glory to God in the Highest,
    and on earth peace,
    good will towards men.
We praise Thee! We bless Thee! We worship Thee! We glorify Thee!
    We give thanks to Thee for Thy great glory!
O Lord, heavenly King,
    God the Father Almighty!
O Lord, the only-begotten Son Jesus Christ
    and the Holy Spirit!

O Lord God, Lamb of God, Son of the Father,
> Who takest away the sins of the world,
> have mercy on us!

Thou that takest away the sins of the world,
> receive our prayer.

Thou that sittest at the right hand of God the Father
> have mercy on us!

For Thou alone art holy, Thou only art Lord,
> Thou only, O Jesus Christ, art most high
> in the glory of God the Father. Amen!

Every night will I give thanks to Thee
> and praise Thy name for ever and ever!

Lord, Thou hast been our refuge
> from generation to generation!

I said, Lord be merciful to me,
> heal my soul for I have sinned against Thee.

Lord, I flee unto Thee.
> Teach me to do Thy will,
> for Thou art my God.

For with Thee is the fountain of life,
> and in Thy light shall we see light.

O continue forth Thy mercy
> upon those who know Thee!

Grant, Lord, that we may be kept this night
> without sin!

Blessed art Thou, Lord God of our fathers,

and praised and glorified
be Thy name forever. Amen!
Let Thy mercy, Lord, be upon us,
as we have set our hope on Thee.
Blessed art Thou, Lord,
teach me Thy statutes!
Blessed art Thou, Master,
make me to understand Thy
commandments!
Blessed art Thou, Holy One,
enlighten me with Thy precepts!
Thy mercy, Lord, endures forever!
O despise not the works of Thy hands!
To Thee belongs worship! To Thee belongs
praise!
To Thee belongs glory:
To the Father, and to the Son, and to the Holy
Spirit,
now and ever, and unto ages of ages. Amen!

The Symbol of Faith

I believe in one God, the Father almighty, Maker of heaven and earth, and of all things visible and invisible.

And in one Lord Jesus Christ, the Son of God, the only-begotten, begotten of the Father before all ages. Light of Light; true God of true God; begotten, not made; of one essence with the Father, by whom all things were made; who for us men and for our salvation came down from heaven, and was incarnate of the Holy Spirit and the Virgin Mary, and became man. And He was crucified for us under Pontius Pilate, and suffered, and was buried. And the third day He rose again, according to the Scriptures, and ascended into heaven, and sits at the right hand of the Father; and He shall come again with glory to judge the living and the dead; whose Kingdom shall have no end.

And in the Holy Spirit, the Lord, the Giver of Life, who proceeds from the Father; who with the Father and the Son together is worshipped and glorified; who spoke by the prophets. In one Holy, Catholic, and Apostolic Church. I acknowledge one baptism for the remission of sins. I look for the resurrection of the dead, and the life of the world to come. Amen.

NOTE: In churches, the appointed Compline Canon to the Theotokos is sung from the Octoechos at this point.

When Compline is read privately, one or more Canons and/or an Akathist Hymn is sung instead.

It is the tradition of the Russian Church that those preparing to receive the Holy Mysteries (Communion) read at least three Canons and one Akathist Hymn the evening before. Some read the Canon of Preparation at this point.

Whenever a Canon is sung, the following is sung to the same melody as the Irmos of the Canon. If there is no Canon, it is either read or sung to the 8th Tone.

It is truly meet to bless you, O Theotokos, ever-blessed and most pure, and the Mother of our God. More honorable than the Cherubim, and more glorious beyond compare than the Seraphim: without defilement you gave birth to God the Word: true Theotokos, we magnify you.

The reader continues:

>Holy God! Holy Mighty! Holy Immortal! Have mercy on us! *(Repeat three times.)*
>Glory to the Father, and to the Son, and to the Holy Spirit,
>>now and ever, and unto ages of ages. Amen.
>
>O Most Holy Trinity, have mercy on us!

Lord, cleanse us from our sins! Master, pardon
   our transgressions! Holy One, visit and
   heal our infirmities, for Thy name's sake!
Lord, have mercy! *(Repeat three times.)*
Glory to the Father, and to the Son, and to the
   Holy Spirit,
      now and ever, and unto ages of ages. Amen.

Our Father who art in heaven, hallowed be Thy name. Thy Kingdom come. Thy will be done, on earth as it is in heaven. Give us this day our daily bread; and forgive us our trespasses, as we forgive those who trespass against us; and lead us not into temptation, but deliver us from evil.

If there is a priest, he gives the usual exclamation.

After saying AMEN!, the reader reads the appropriate TROPARIA:

Sunday Evening

We, the unworthy, ever pray to you, Supreme Commanders of the Heavenly Hosts: shelter us, through your prayers, with the protective wings of your glory. Keep us who fall down with fervor and cry: deliver us from misfortunes, for you command the powers on high.

O God of our fathers, Who dealest ever with us according to Thy meekness: take not Thy mercy from us, but direct our lives in peace through their prayers.

Thy Church has been adorned with a robe of fine purple linen—the blood of Thy Martyrs throughout the world, O Christ God. She therefore cries to Thee: send Thy mercies upon Thy people, give peace to Thy community and great mercy to our souls.

> Glory to the Father, and to the Son, and to the Holy Spirit:

O Christ, give rest to the souls of Thy servants with the saints, where there is no sickness, sorrow or sighing, but everlasting life.

> Now and ever and unto ages of ages. Amen.

Grant us Thy peace, O Lord, through the prayers of all the saints and the Theotokos. Have mercy on us, for Thou alone art compassionate.

Monday Evening

The just man is remembered with praises. For you, O Forerunner, the witness of the Lord is sufficient. You truly showed yourself more honorable than the prophets, for you were made worthy to baptize in the streams the One Whom you proclaimed. Having gladly suffered for the truth, you proclaimed to those in Hades the true God Who has revealed Himself in the flesh, taken away the sin of the world and given us great mercy.

O God of our Fathers ...

Thy Church has been adorned ...

> Glory to the Father ...

O Christ, give rest ...

> Now and ever ...

Grant us Thy peace, O Lord, ...

Tuesday Evening

O Lord, save Thy people, and bless Thine inheritance. Grant victories to the Orthodox Christians over their adversaries; and by the virtue of Thy Cross, preserve Thy habitation.

O God of our Fathers ...

Thy Church has been adorned ...

Glory to the Father ...

O Christ, give rest ...
> Now and ever ...

Grant us Thy peace, O Lord, ...

Wednesday Evening

O holy Apostles, pray to our merciful God, that He grant remission of sins to our souls.

The truth of things revealed you to your flock as a rule of faith, an Icon of meekness and a teacher of abstinence. You thus reached the heights through humility and wealth through poverty. O holy hierarch, father Nicholas, pray to Christ God for the salvation of our souls.

O God of our Fathers ...

Thy Church has been adorned ...
> Glory to the Father ...

O Christ, give rest ...
> Now and ever ...

Grant us Thy peace, O Lord, ...

Thursday Evening

The same as Tuesday evening.

Friday Evening

We pray to you, apostles, martyrs and prophets, hierarchs, venerable and righteous ones, who have fought the good fight and kept the faith: having boldness before the Savior, pray to Him Who is good for the salvation of our souls.

> Glory to the Father, and to the Son, and to the Holy Spirit:
> now and ever, and unto ages of ages. Amen.

To Thee, Lord, the Planter of Creation, the universe offers the God-bearing Martyrs as the first-fruits of nature. Through their prayers and the Theotokos, Most Merciful One, keep Thy Church and Thy people in profound peace.

Saturday Evening

The Sunday Troparia and Kontakia are read, according to the Tone of the week.

Tone 1

When the stone had been sealed by the Jews; while the soldiers were guarding Thy most pure Body; Thou didst rise on the third day, O Savior, granting life to the world. The powers of heaven therefore cried to Thee, O Giver of Life: Glory to Thy resurrection, O Christ! Glory to Thy Kingdom! Glory to Thy dispensation, O Thou who lovest mankind.

> Glory to the Father, and to the Son, and to the Holy Spirit,
> now and ever, and unto ages of ages. Amen.

As God, Thou didst rise from the tomb in glory, raising the world with Thyself. Human nature praises Thee as God, for death has vanished! Adam exults, O Master! Eve rejoices, for she is freed from bondage, and cries to Thee: Thou art the Giver of Resurrection to all, O Christ!

Tone 2

When Thou didst descend to death, O Life Immortal, Thou didst slay hell with the splendor of Thy Godhead! And when from the depths Thou didst raise the dead, all the powers of heaven cried out: O Giver of Life! Christ our God! Glory to Thee!

> Glory to the Father.... Now and ever....

Hell became afraid, O Almighty Savior, seeing the miracle of Thy resurrection from the tomb! The dead arose! Creation, with Adam, beheld this and rejoiced with Thee! And the world, O my Savior, praises Thee forever.

Tone 3

Let the heavens rejoice! Let the earth be glad! For the Lord has shown strength with His arm! He has trampled down death by death! He has become the firstborn of the dead! He has delivered us from the depths of hell, and has granted the world great mercy!

> Glory to the Father.... Now and ever....

On this day Thou didst rise from the tomb, O Merciful One, leading us from the gates of death. On this day Adam exults as Eve rejoices; with the prophets and patriarchs they unceasingly praise the divine majesty of Thy power!

Tone 4

When the women disciples of the Lord learned from the angel the joyous message of Thy Resurrection; they cast away the ancestral curse and elatedly told the apostles: Death is overthrown! Christ God is risen, granting the world great mercy.

> Glory to the Father.... Now and ever....

My Savior and Redeemer as God rose from the tomb and delivered the earthborn from their chains. He has shattered the gates of hell, and as Master, He has risen on the third day!

Tone 5

Let us, the faithful, praise and worship the Word, coeternal with the Father and the Spirit, born for our salvation from the Virgin; for He willed to be lifted up on the Cross in the flesh, to endure death, and to raise the dead by His glorious Resurrection.

> Glory to the Father.... Now and ever....

Thou didst descend into hell, O my Savior, shattering its gates as Almighty; resurrecting the dead as Creator, and destroying the sting of death. Thou hast delivered Adam from the curse, O Lover of Man, and we all cry to Thee: O Lord, save us!

Tone 6

The angelic powers were at Thy tomb; the guards became as dead men. Mary stood by Thy grave, seeking Thy most pure Body. Thou didst capture hell, not being tempted by it. Thou didst come to the Virgin, granting life. O Lord who didst rise from the dead: glory to Thee!

Glory to the Father.... Now and ever....

When Christ God, the Giver of Life, raised all of the dead from the valleys of misery with His mighty hand, He bestowed resurrection on the human race. He is the Savior of all, the Resurrection, the Life, and the God of all.

Tone 7

By Thy Cross, Thou didst destroy death! To the thief, Thou didst open Paradise! For the myrrhbearers, Thou didst change weeping into joy! And Thou didst command Thy disciples, O Christ God, to proclaim that Thou art risen, granting the world great mercy!

Glory to the Father.... Now and ever....

The dominion of death can no longer hold men captive, for Christ descended, shattering and destroying its powers! Hell is bound, while the prophets rejoice and cry: The Savior has come to those in faith! Enter, you faithful, into the Resurrection!

Tone 8

Thou didst descend from on high, O Merciful One! Thou didst accept the three-day burial to free us from our sufferings! O Lord, our Life and Resurrection: glory to Thee!

Glory to the Father.... Now and ever....

By rising from the tomb, Thou didst raise the dead and resurrect Adam. Eve exults in Thy Resurrection, and the world celebrates Thy rising from the dead, O greatly Merciful One!

NOTE: On the eve of Great Feasts of the Lord or the Theotokos, the Troparion and Kontakion of the Feast are read.

After the Troparia, the reader continues:

Lord, have mercy! *(Repeat forty times.)*

A Prayer of Saint Basil the Great

O Christ God, Who art worshipped and glorified at every place and time; Who art long-suffering, most merciful and compassionate; Who lovest the righteous and art merciful to sinners; Who callest all to salvation with the promise of good things to come: receive, Lord, the prayers we now offer, and direct our lives in the way of Thy commandments. Sanctify our souls, cleanse our bodies, correct our thoughts, purify our minds and deliver us from all affliction, evil and illness. Surround us with Thy holy angels, that guarded and instructed by their forces, we may reach unity of faith and the understanding of Thine unapproachable glory: for blessed art Thou unto ages of ages. Amen.

Lord, have mercy! *(Repeat three times.)*

> Glory to the Father, and to the Son, and to the Holy Spirit,
> now and ever, and unto ages of ages. Amen.

More honorable than the Cherubim, and more glorious beyond compare than the Seraphim: without defilement you gave birth to God the Word: true Theotokos, we magnify you!

When a priest is serving, the reader concludes:

Bless, father, in the name of the Lord!

The priest exclaims:

O God, be gracious to us and bless us! Shine Thy countenance upon us, and have mercy on us!

In the absence of a priest, a layman says:

"Through the prayers of our holy fathers, Lord Jesus Christ, our God, have mercy on us. Amen".

In either case, the reader, after saying "Amen", continues with the following:

NOTE: During Great Lent the Lenten Prayer of Saint Ephraim is recited at this point of most services during the week (not on Saturday or Sunday). It is also appropriate for Morning Prayers and the Prayers Before Sleep on the same days.

Prayer of Saint Ephraim

O Lord and Master of my life! Take from me the spirit of sloth, despair, lust of power and idle talk. *(Prostration)*

But give rather the spirit of chastity, humility, patience, and love to Thy servant. *(Prostration)*

Yea, O Lord and King! Grant me to see my own transgressions and not to judge my brother, for blessed art Thou, unto ages of ages. *(Prostration)*

O God, cleanse me a sinner. *(Repeat twelve times.)*

(Then the entire Prayer of Saint Ephraim is read and a single prostration is made at the end.)

Prayer to the Most Holy Theotokos by the Monk Paul

O undefiled, immaculate, incorrupt and most pure Lady, the pure Virgin Bride of God! Through your most glorious birth-giving, you united God the Word to mankind and joined our fallen human nature to the heavenly. You are the only hope of the hopeless, the aid of the embattled a ready help to those who run to you and a refuge for all Christians. Do not turn away from me who am sinful and vile, even though I have made myself totally useless through defiled thoughts, words and deeds, and my mind has become enslaved to the lazy pleasures of this life. As Mother of the God Who loves mankind, have pity on me, a prodigal sinner, in that same love for mankind. Receive the prayer I offer to you with defiled lips and pray to your Son, our Master and Lord, with your maternal boldness. May He open even to me the goodness of His deep love for mankind. May He overlook my countless transgressions, turn me to repentance and make me an experienced accomplisher of His commandments. Stand by me always in your mercy, compassion and love of good. Be my fervent intercessor and help in this life, driving off the assaults of enemies and guiding me to salvation. Guard my wretched soul at the time of my death, driving away the dark forms of the evil demons. Deliver me from eternal torments at the Day of Judgment and reveal me an heir of the inexpressible glory of your Son and our God. May I receive this, my Lady most glorious Theotokos, through your help and intercession: through the Grace and love for mankind of your only-begotten Son, our Lord, God and Savior Jesus Christ, to Whom belong all glory, honor and worship, with His Father Who is without beginning, and His most holy, good and life-creating Spirit, now and ever, and unto ages of ages. Amen.

A Prayer to Our Lord Jesus Christ
 by the Monk Antiochus

As we prepare for sleep, Master, grant rest to our bodies and souls. Keep us from the dark sleep of sin and from every dark and passionate pleasure of the night. Still the impulses of passions and put out the flaming arrows which the Evil One looses deceitfully against us. Still the rebellions of the flesh and put to sleep our worldly and material reasonings. O God, grant us an alert mind, chaste thoughts, a sober heart, and a light sleep, free of every satanic dream. Raise us at the time of prayer confirmed in Thy commandments —the memory of Thy judgments firmly in us. Grant that we may glorify Thee throughout this night, singing, blessing and glorifying Thy most honorable and majestic name: the Father, the Son, and the Holy Spirit, now and ever, and unto ages of ages. Amen.

NOTE: In churches, Compline concludes at this point with brief prayers and a Litany. (See the BOOK OF HOURS)

When read privately, Compline moves into PRAYERS BEFORE SLEEP, beginning with the Troparia: "Have mercy on us, O Lord, have mercy on us...."

BEFORE SLEEP

Lord Jesus Christ, Son of God, through the prayers of Thy most pure Mother and all the saints, have mercy on us. Amen.

Glory to Thee, our God, glory to Thee!

O Heavenly King, the Comforter, the Spirit of Truth, Who art everywhere and fillest all things. Treasury of blessings and Giver of life: come and abide in us, and cleanse us from every impurity, and save our souls, O Good One.

Holy God! Holy Mighty! Holy Immortal! Have mercy on us! *(Repeat three times.)*

Glory to the Father, and to the Son, and to the Holy Spirit, now and ever and unto ages of ages. Amen.

O Most Holy Trinity: have mercy on us. Lord, cleanse us from our sins. Master, pardon our transgressions. Holy One, visit and heal our infirmities for Thy Name's sake.

Lord, have mercy! *(Repeat three times.)*

Glory to the Father, and to the Son, and to the Holy Spirit, now and ever and unto ages of ages. Amen.

Our Father Who art in heaven, hallowed be Thy name. Thy Kingdom come. Thy will be done, on earth as it is in heaven. Give us this day our daily bread; and forgive us our trespasses, as we forgive those who trespass against us; and lead us not into temptation, but deliver us from evil.

If there is a priest, he adds the usual exclamation.

After the AMEN, the following Troparia are sung (Tone 6) or read:

Have mercy on us, O Lord, have mercy on us, for laying aside all excuse, we sinners offer to Thee, as to our Master, this supplication: have mercy on us.

Glory to the Father, and to the Son, and to the Holy Spirit:

O Lord, have mercy on us, for in Thee have we put our trust. Do not be angry with us, nor remember our iniquities, but look down on us even now, since Thou art compassionate, and deliver us from our enemies; for Thou art our God and we are Thy people; we are all the work of Thy hands, and we call on Thy name.

Now and ever, and unto ages of ages. Amen.

O blessed Theotokos, open the doors of compassion to us whose hope is in you, that we may not perish but be delivered from adversity through you, who are the salvation of the Christian people.

Lord, have mercy! *(Repeat twelve times.)*

1st Prayer, to God the Father
by Saint Macarius the Great

O Eternal God and King of all Creation, Who hast granted me to reach this hour: forgive the sins I have committed this day in deed, word and thought. Cleanse, O Lord, my humble soul from every defilement of flesh and spirit. Grant, Lord, that I may pass through this night in peace. When I rise from my humble bed, may I please Thy most holy Name all the days of my life and trample under foot the physical and bodiless enemies that wage war against me. Deliver me, Lord, from vain thoughts which defile me and from evil lusts. For Thine is the Kingdom and the Power and the Glory, of the Father, and of the Son, and of the Holy Spirit, now and ever and unto ages of ages. Amen.

2nd Prayer, to Our Lord Jesus Christ by Saint Antiochus

Almighty Word of the Father, Jesus Christ, Who art perfect: never abandon me, Thy servant, for Thy great mercy's sake, but ever abide in me. O Jesus, Good Shepherd of Thy sheep, do not deliver me to the serpent's rebellion! Do not abandon me to Satan's will, for the seed of corruption is within me! Instead, O Lord God the Adored, Holy King Jesus Christ, keep me while I sleep by Thy unwavering Light, Thy Holy Spirit by Whom Thou didst sanctify Thy disciples. O Lord, grant to me, Thine unworthy servant, salvation on my bed. Enlighten my mind with the light of understanding Thy Holy Gospel; my soul with the love of Thy Cross; my heart with the purity of Thy Word; my body with Thy passionless Passion. Keep my thoughts with Thy humility and raise me at the right time to glorify Thee. For Thou art most glorified, with Thine unoriginate Father and Thy most Holy Spirit forever. Amen.

3rd Prayer, to the Holy Spirit

O Lord, the Heavenly King, the Comforter, the Spirit of Truth: have compassion and mercy on me, Thy sinful servant! Absolve me, who am unworthy. Forgive all the sins I have committed this day both in my humanity and my inhumanity, behaving worse than beasts in sins voluntary and involuntary, known and unknown, from my youth, from evil suggestions, haste and despondency. If I have sworn by Thy name or blasphemed it in thought; if I have reproached anyone or become angered by something; or slandered or saddened anyone in my anger; or have lied, or slept unnecessarily; or a beggar has come to me and I have despised him; or have saddened my brother or quarrelled with him; or have judged someone; or have allowed myself to become haughty, proud or angry; or, when standing in prayer, my mind has been shaken by the wickedness of this world; or have entertained depraved thoughts; or have over-eaten, over-drunk or laughed mindlessly; or have had evil thoughts or seen the beauty of someone and been wounded by it in my heart; or have spoken inappropriately; or have laughed at my brother's sins when my own transgressions are countless; or have been indifferent to prayer; or have done any other evil that I can not remember—for I have done all this and more: have mercy, O Master, my Creator, on me, Thy despondent and unworthy servant! Absolve, remit and forgive me, in Thy goodness and love for mankind, that I, who am prodigal, sinful and wretched, may lie down in peace and find sleep and rest May I worship, hymn and praise Thy most honorable Name, with the Father and His only-begotten Son, now and ever and unto ages of ages. Amen.

4th Prayer, of Saint Macarius the Great

What can I bring Thee? With what can I repay Thee, O Immortal King, the bestower of great gifts, O generous Lord, the Lover of mankind? Though I have been lazy in pleasing Thee and have done no good, Thou hast brought me to the end of this day, ordering the conversion and salvation of my soul. Be merciful towards me, a sinner devoid of any good deeds. Raise up my fallen soul, defiled by immeasurable sins. Remove from me every evil thought of this visible life. Forgive, O only Sinless One, all the sins I have committed against Thee this day, in knowledge or in ignorance, in word, deed or thought or through any of my senses. Covering me Thyself, protect me from every assault of the enemy through Thy divine Power, inexpressible Love for mankind and Strength. Cleanse, O God, cleanse the multitude of my sins. Be pleased, O Lord, to deliver me from the snares of the Evil One, and save my passionate soul. When Thou comest in glory, illumine me with the light of Thy countenance. May I fall uncondemned into a sleep free of apparitions. Keep the thoughts of Thy servant untroubled, and keep far from me every satanic activity. Enlighten the reason-endowed eyes of my heart, that I fall not into the sleep of death. Send to me an angel of peace, the guide and guardian of my soul and body, that he may deliver me from my enemies. Then, when I arise from my bed, I shall offer Thee prayers of thanksgiving. Yea, Lord, hear me, Thy sinful servant, impoverished in will and conscience. Grant that I may learn from Thy words when I arise. Cause Thy Angels to drive demonic despondency far from me. May I bless Thy holy Name and praise and glorify Mary, the most pure Theotokos, whom Thou hast given to us sinners as an intercessor. Receive her as she prays for us. We know that she imitates Thy love for mankind and never ceases to pray. Through her intercessions, the Sign of the Precious Cross and for the sake of all Thy saints, O Jesus Christ our God, have mercy on my wretched soul, for Thou art Holy and most glorified unto ages of ages. Amen.

5th Prayer

O Lord our God, forgive all the sins I have committed this day in word, deed and thought, for Thou art good and lovest mankind. Grant me a peaceful sleep, free of restlessness. Send Thy Guardian Angel to protect and keep me from all harm. For Thou art the Guardian of our souls and bodies, and to Thee we ascribe glory, to the Father, and to the Son, and to the Holy Spirit, now and ever and unto ages of ages. Amen.

6th Prayer

O Lord our God, in Whom we believe and upon Whose Name we call more than any other name: grant relief to our souls and bodies as we go to sleep. Keep us from every fantasy and dark pleasure. Halt the rushing of passions and quench the fiery arousals of the flesh. Grant us to live chastely in word and deed. Having embraced a virtuous life, may we not fall away from Thy promised blessings, for blessed art Thou for ever. Amen.

7th Prayer, by Saint John Chrysostom

Prayers of Supplication, corresponding to the twenty-four hours of day and night.

For the Day

Lord, exclude me not from Thy heavenly blessings.
Lord, deliver me from eternal torments.
Lord, whether I have sinned in mind or thought, word or deed, forgive me.
Lord, deliver me from all ignorance, forgetfulness, cowardice, and stone-like insensitivity.
Lord, deliver me from every temptation.

Lord, enlighten my heart which evil desires have darkened.

Lord, as a man I have sinned: as a gracious God, have mercy on me, seeing the weakness of my soul.

Lord, send Thy Grace to my aid, that I may glorify Thy holy name.

Lord Jesus Christ, inscribe me, Thy servant, in the book of life, and grant me a good end.

Lord, my God, even though I have done nothing good before Thee, grant by Thy Grace that I may make a good beginning.

Lord, sprinkle the dew of Thy Grace into my heart.

Lord of Heaven and earth, remember me, Thy sinful, shameful and impure servant, in Thy Kingdom. Amen.

For the Night

Lord, accept me in penitence.

Lord, abandon me not.

Lord, lead me not into temptation.

Lord, grant me good thoughts.

Lord, grant me tears, the remembrance of death and compunction.

Lord, grant me the thought of confessing my sins.
Lord, grant me humility, chastity and obedience.
Lord, grant me patience, courage and meekness.
Lord, cause the root of good to dwell in me—Thy fear in my heart.
Lord, grant that I may love Thee with all my soul and mind and to do Thy will in all things.
Lord, protect me from certain people, demons and passions, and from any other unseemly thing.
Lord, I know that Thou doest as Thou wilt: may Thy will be in me, a sinner, for blessed art Thou for ever. Amen.

8th Prayer, to our Lord Jesus Christ

O Lord Jesus Christ the Son of God, for the sake of Thy most honorable Mother, Thy bodiless Angels, Thy Prophet, Forerunner and Baptist, the Divinely inspired Apostles, the bright and victorious Martyrs, the venerable and God-bearing Fathers and all the Saints: deliver me from this present assault of the devil. Yea, O Lord my Creator, Who desirest not the death of the sinner, but that he should return to Thee and live: grant repentance to me, wretched and unworthy. Snatch me from the jaws of the consuming serpent, its mouth opened to devour me and take me down to hell alive. Yea, my Lord and my

Comfort, Who didst put on corruptible flesh for my wretched sake: deliver me from wretchedness and bring comfort to my wretched soul. Implant in my heart the accomplishment of Thy precepts, the abandonment of evil deeds and the obtainment of Thy blessings. In Thee, O Lord, have I trusted: save me!

9th Prayer, to the Most Holy Theotokos by Peter, the Studite monk

Before you, the Most Pure Mother of God, I who am wretched fall down and pray: you know, O Queen that I sin constantly and anger your Son and my God. No matter how often I repent, I appear a liar before God, and repent with trembling. Can God shake me and I do those same things again an hour later? Knowing this, my Mistress, O Lady Theotokos, I pray: have mercy on me, strengthen me and grant that I may do good. You know, my Lady Theotokos, that I abhor my evil deeds and love the Law of my God with all my mind. But, most pure Lady, I do not know how I can love what I abhor and turn away from what is good. Do not allow my will to be done, Most Pure One, for it is not appropriate. May the will of your Son and my God be done. May He save and enlighten me, and give me the Grace of His Holy Spirit, in order that I might stop sinning from this time on and live the remainder of my life in obedience to your Son, to

Whom belongs all glory, honor and majesty, with His Father Who is without beginning, and His Most Holy, good and life-creating Spirit, now and ever and unto ages of ages. Amen.

10th Prayer, to the Most Holy Theotokos

O Good Mother of the Good King, most pure and blessed Mary the Theotokos: pour out the mercy of your Son and our God on my passionate soul. Direct me towards good deeds through your prayers, that I may pass through the remainder of my life without stain, and find Paradise through you, O Virgin Theotokos who alone are pure and blessed.

11th Prayer, to the Holy Guardian Angel

Angel of Christ, my holy guardian, the protector of my soul and body: forgive me for all the sins I have committed this day. Deliver me from all the evil of my militant Enemy, that I may not anger my God by any sin. Pray for me, your sinful and unworthy servant, that you may show me worthy of the goodness and mercy of the All-Holy Trinity, the Mother of my Lord Jesus Christ and all the Saints. Amen.

Then this Kontakion to the Theotokos

O victorious leader of triumphant hosts! We your servants, delivered from evil, sing our grateful thanks to you, O Theotokos! As you possess invincible might, set us free from every calamity so that we may sing: Rejoice, O unwedded Bride!

Most glorious ever-Virgin Mother of Christ our God, bear our prayer to your Son and our God, that through you He may save our souls!

All my hope I place in you, O Mother of God: keep me under your protection!

Virgin Theotokos, do not despise me a sinner who craves your help and intercession. My soul hopes in you, have mercy on me!

Also the Prayer of Saint Ioannikios

My Hope is the Father; my Refuge is the Son; my Protection is the Holy Spirit: O Holy Trinity, glory to Thee!

It is truly meet to bless you, O Theotokos, ever blessed and most pure, and the Mother of our God. More honorable than the Cherubim, and more glorious beyond compare than the Seraphim: without defilement you gave birth to God the Word: true Theotokos, we magnify you!

Glory to the Father, and to the Son, and to the Holy Spirit, now and ever and unto ages of ages. Amen.

Lord, have mercy! *(Repeat three times.)*

Lord, bless!

Lord Jesus Christ, Son of God, for the sake of the prayers of Thy most pure Mother, our venerable and God-bearing fathers and all the saints, save me, a sinner. Amen.

A Prayer of Saint John of Damascus, said signaling towards the bed

O Master Who lovest mankind, is this bed to be my coffin? Or wilt Thou enlighten my wretched soul with another day? Behold: before me lies the coffin, before me stands death! O Lord, I fear Thy judgment and the endless torments, yet I cease not to do evil. I always anger Thee, my Lord God, and Thy most pure Mother, all the heavenly hosts and my holy Guardian Angel. I know, Lord, that I am unworthy of Thy love for mankind. Indeed, I am worthy of every condemnation and torment. Yet, Lord, save me whether I want it or not! When Thou savest the righteous, it is no great thing. When Thou hast mercy on the pure, it causes no wonder, for they are worthy of Thy mercy. Astound us with Thy mercy towards me, a sinner. Reveal in this manner Thy love for mankind, that my wickedness may not overcome Thine inexpressible goodness and mercy. As Thou wilt, order my life!

Wishing to lie down on your bed, say:

Enlighten my eyes, Christ—God, that I fall not asleep to death and that my enemy may not say of me: I have overcome him.

Glory to the Father, and to the Son, and to the Holy Spirit:

Be the Helper of my soul, O God, for I walk among many snares. Deliver me from them, O Good One, and save me, for Thou lovest mankind.

Now and ever and unto ages of ages. Amen.

Let us ever hymn the most glorious Mother of God, who is holier than the Holy Angels. With heart and lips let us confess that she is the Theotokos, for she truly bore God incarnate for us and prays ceaselessly for our souls.

BEFORE SLEEP

Kiss your Cross. Then, make the Sign of the Cross over your bed, from head to foot and either side, saying the Prayer to the Precious Cross:

Let God arise and let His enemies be scattered! Let those who hate Him flee from before His face! As smoke vanishes, so let them vanish. As wax melts before the fire, so let sinners perish before the face of those who love God and sign themselves with the Sign of the Cross and say joyfully: rejoice, most precious and life-creating Cross of the Lord, which chases demons away through the power of our Lord Jesus Christ Who was nailed to you, descended into hell and, having trampled down the power of the devil, gave to us His precious Cross for the routing of all enemies. Help me for ever, most precious and life-creating Cross of the Lord, with the Holy Lady Virgin Theotokos and all the Saints. Amen.

Remit, absolve and forgive, O God, all our voluntary and involuntary sins, in word and in deed, in knowledge and in ignorance, in the day or in the night, in mind and in thought! Forgive us everything, for Thou art good and lovest mankind.

O Lord Who lovest mankind, forgive those who hate and wrong us. Do good to those who do good. Grant to our brethren and relatives all petitions for salvation and eternal life. Visit the afflicted and heal them. Guide those at sea. Travel with travellers. Join the Orthodox Christians in battle. Grant remission of sins to those who serve us and are kind to us. Have mercy, according to Thy great mercy, on those who have asked us to pray for them, unworthy though we be. Remember, Lord, our fathers and brethren who have fallen asleep before us, and give them rest under the light of Thy countenance. Remember, Lord, our captive brethren, and deliver them from every misfortune. Remember, Lord, those who bear fruit and do good works in Thy holy churches, and grant them all their petitions for salvation and eternal life. Remember us also, Lord, Thy humble, sinful, and unworthy servants. Enlighten our minds with the light of Thy reason and direct us onto the path of Thy commandments, through the prayers of our most Pure Lady, the Theotokos and ever-virgin Mary and all Thy Saints, for blessed art Thou unto ages of ages. Amen.

THE THREE CANONS

A tradition has developed in the Church of reading three (sometimes four) Canons the evening before receiving Holy Communion. Many monastic Rules of Prayer prescribe this reading daily. Many Canons have been composed over the years, and certain Canons are prescribed for specific days of the week. We have not attempted to publish a large selection of Canons in the limited space of what is, essentially, a "pocket" Prayer Book. We have provided three of the most commonly used Canons and printed them in the order in which they are traditionally read. This order can also serve as a model for combining other Canons. If these Canons are not read during Compline (p. 37), they are preceded by the Opening Prayers and Psalm 50.

THE THREE CANONS
ODE 1 (Tone 6)

Irmos: Treading over the floor of the sea as over dry land, and seeing their pursuer Pharaoh drown, Israel cried out: Let us sing to God a song of victory!

Canon of Repentance

Have mercy on me, O God, have mercy on me!

Sinful and burdened, I now approach Thee, my Master and my God. I dare not look up towards heaven, but simply pray, saying: grant me, Lord, the sense to weep bitterly over my deeds.

Have mercy on me, O God, have mercy on me!

O woe is me, a sinner! I am the most wretched of men! There is no repentance in me! Grant me tears, Lord, that I may weep bitterly over my deeds.

Have mercy on me, O God, have mercy on me!

O senseless and wretched man, you are destroying your life in laziness! Think about your life and turn to the Lord God, weeping bitterly over your deeds.

Most Holy Theotokos, save us!

O most pure Mother of God, look on me, a sinner, and deliver me from the snares of the devil. Direct me onto the path of repentance, that I may weep bitterly over my deeds.

Canon to the Theotokos

Most Holy Theotokos, save us!

Beset by many temptations, I run to you, seeking salvation. Save me from burdens and evils, O Virgin Mother of the Word.

Most Holy Theotokos, save us!

The increase of passions troubles me, filling my soul with great despondency. Still it, O Maiden, with the stillness of your Son and God, O All-Undefiled One.

Most Holy Theotokos, save us!

I pray you, O Virgin who bore our Savior and God, deliver me from terrors! I run to you now, laying before you my soul and my thoughts.

Most Holy Theotokos, save us!

O only Mother of God, grant me, who am afflicted in body and soul, divine visitation and your own concern, for you are good and gave birth to the Good One.

Canon to the Guardian Angel

Lord Jesus Christ, my God, have mercy on me!

Grant, O Savior, that Thy servant may worthily hymn and praise the bodiless Angel who is my instructor and guardian.

Holy Angel of the Lord, my guardian, pray to God for me, a sinner!

I lie alone in folly and laziness, O my instructor and Guardian. Do not leave me to perish!

Glory to the Father and to the Son, and to the Holy Spirit:

Direct my mind, through your prayers, to accomplish the commandments of God, that I may receive from God the remission of my sins. Teach me to hate evil, I pray you.

Now and ever, and unto ages of ages. Amen.

With my Guardian Angel, O Virgin, pray to the Benefactor for your servant. Teach me to accomplish the commandments of your Son and my Creator.

ODE 3

Irmos: None is holy as Thou, O Lord my God! Thou hast raised the strength of Thy faithful, O Good One, and made us stand firmly on the rock of Thy confession.

Canon of Repentance

Have mercy on me, O God, have mercy on me!

When the thrones will be set up for the dread Judgment, the deeds of all men will be recalled. Alas for the sinners who will be sent to torment! Knowing this, my soul, repent of your evil deeds!

Have mercy on me, O God, have mercy on me!

The righteous shall rejoice, but sinners shall lament. No one will be able to help us at that moment—our deeds will condemn us! Before the end comes, repent of your evil deeds!

Have mercy on me, O God, have mercy on me!

Woe is me, a great sinner! I have defiled myself in deed and thought and cannot even shed a single tear in my hard-heartedness. Free yourself from the earth, my soul, and repent of your evil deeds.

Most Holy Theotokos, save us!

Your Son calls, O Lady, and teaches us what is good. Yet I, a sinner, always flee from good. Have mercy on me, nevertheless, O merciful one, that I may repent of my evil deeds.

Canon to the Theotokos

Most Holy Theotokos, save us!

I hold you as the Intercessor and Protection of my life, O Virgin Birth-Giver of God. Pilot me to your haven, O Cause of good things, O only all-hymned Support of the faithful.

Most Holy Theotokos, save us!

I pray, O Virgin: dispel the storm of my sorrows and spiritual turmoil. You are the Bride of God who bore the Origin of stillness and alone are most pure.

Most Holy Theotokos, save us!

Pour a wealth of generosity for all, O you who bore the Benefactor, the Cause of all good. You can do anything, for God has blessed you, the Bearer of Christ Who is mighty in strength.

Most Holy Theotokos, save us!

Help me, O Virgin, for I am cruelly tried by severe illness and painful afflictions. I know, Ever-Undefiled One, that you are an inexhaustible and generous treasury of healings.

Canon to the Guardian Angel

Holy Angel of the Lord, my Guardian, pray to God for me, a sinner!

I have laid all my thoughts and my soul before you, my Guardian. Deliver me from every assault of the Enemy.

Holy Angel of the Lord, my Guardian, pray to God for me, a sinner!

The Enemy humiliates and oppresses me and teaches me always to do his will. But you, my Instructor, leave me not to perish!

Glory to the Father, and to the Son, and to the Holy Spirit:

Grant me with thanksgiving and fervor to sing a hymn to my Creator and God and to you my good Guardian Angel. Free me from my oppressive enemies, O my Deliverer.

Now and ever and unto ages of ages. Amen.

Heal, Most Pure One, the most painful wounds of my soul and drive off the enemies that are constantly warring against me.

Lord have mercy! (Repeat three times.)

Sessional Hymn, Tone 6

I think of the Dread Day and weep over my evil deeds. How shall I answer the immortal King? Or how shall a prodigal like me dare to look up at the judge? O compassionate Father, only-begotten Son, and Holy Spirit: have mercy on me!

Glory to the Father, and to the Son, and to the Holy Spirit:

Sessional Hymn, Tone 2

In fervent love I cry to you, O Guardian of my soul, my all-holy Angel: protect me and keep me always from the entrapment of the evil one. Direct me to the heavenly life, enlightening, illumining, and strengthening me.

Now and ever and unto ages of ages. Amen.

Kontakion, Tone 6

Steadfast protectress of Christians, constant advocate before the Creator: do not despise the cry of us sinners, but in your goodness come speedily to help us who call on you in faith. Hasten to hear our petition and to intercede for us, O Theotokos, for you always protect those who honor you.

ODE 4

Irmos: "Christ is my strength, my God and my Lord"— the sacred Church reverently sings with a mighty voice, rejoicing in the Lord.

Canon of Repentance

Have mercy on me, O God, have mercy on me!

Our present path is wide and conducive to pleasures, but bitter will the Last Day be when the soul will part from the body. O man, beware of those pleasures, for the sake of the Kingdom of God.

Have mercy on me, O God, have mercy on me!

Why do you mistreat the poor? Why do you withhold the worker's pay? Why do you not love your brother? Why do you pursue lust and pride? Abandon all that, my soul, and repent for the sake of the Kingdom of God.

Have mercy on me, O God, have mercy on me!

O foolish man! How long will you bustle like a bee, gathering your wealth? It will soon perish like dust and ashes. Seek rather the Kingdom of God.

Most Holy Theotokos, save us!

Have mercy on me a sinner, O Lady Theotokos, and strengthen me in virtues. Protect me, so that insolent death may not seize me unprepared, and bring me, O Virgin, to the Kingdom of God.

Canon to the Theotokos

Most Holy Theotokos, save us!

O Bride of God, who bore the Lord Pilot, still the tumult of my passions and the storm of my transgressions.

Most Holy Theotokos, save us!

Grant me the abyss of your kindness, upon which I call, O you who gave birth to the Compassionate One, the Savior of those who hymn you.

Most Holy Theotokos, save us!

Enjoying your gifts, O Pure One, we sing a hymn of thanksgiving to you whom we know to be the Mother of God.

Most Holy Theotokos, save us!

As you love good, O Theotokos, the only ever-Virgin, help me as I lie on my bed of illness and infirmity.

Most Holy Theotokos, save us!

We are delivered from every difficulty, O All-Hymned One, for we have you as our hope, our confirmation, and immovable wall.

Canon to the Guardian Angel

Holy Angel of the Lord, my Guardian, pray to God for me, a sinner!

Pray to God Who loves mankind, my Guardian, and do not abandon me! Keep my life in peace and grant me invincible salvation.

Holy Angel of the Lord, my Guardian, pray to God for me, a sinner!

I received you from God, holy Angel, as a helper and guardian of my life. Free me from all harm, I pray you!

Glory to the Father, and to the Son, and to the Holy Spirit:

Cleanse my vileness with your holiness, my Guardian! May I be excluded from the left side through your prayers and become a partaker of glory.

Now and ever and unto ages of ages. Amen.

I am bewildered by the evils that surround me, Most Pure One. Deliver me from them quickly, for I run only to you.

ODE 5

Irmos: I pray Thee, O Good One: Enlighten with Thy Divine Light the souls which look to Thee from early dawn, that they may know Thee, O Word of God, as the True God Who calls them out from the darkness of sin.

Canon of Repentance

Have mercy on me, O God, have mercy on me!

Remember, wretched man, how you have been enslaved to lies, slander, crime, infirmities, and wild beasts because of your sins. Is this what you wanted, my sinful soul?

Have mercy on me, O God, have mercy on me!

My members tremble, for I have been guilty through all of them: my eyes by seeing, my ears by hearing, my tongue by speaking evil, surrendering my whole self to Gehenna. Is this what you wanted, my sinful soul?

Have mercy on me, O God, have mercy on me!

Thou didst receive the Prodigal and the thief who repented, O Savior. I alone have been weighed down by sinful laziness and submitted to evil deeds. Is this what you wanted my sinful soul?

Most Holy Theotokos, save us!

O Mother of God, the wondrous and swift helper of all mankind, help me, the unworthy, for this is what my sinful soul wants!

Canon to the Theotokos

Most Holy Theotokos, save us!

Fill my heart with joy, O Pure One who bore the Cause of Joy, by giving us your incorruptible joy.

Most Holy Theotokos, save us!

Deliver us from harm, Pure Theotokos who bore the Eternal Redemption and the Peace which passes all understanding.

Most Holy Theotokos, save us!

Lessen the gloom of my transgressions with the enlightenment of your brightness, O Bride of God who bore the divine and eternal Light.

Most Holy Theotokos, save us!

Heal the infirmity of my soul by granting me your visitation, O Pure One, and grant me wholeness by your prayers.

Canon to the Guardian Angel

Holy Angel of the Lord, my Guardian, pray to God for me, a sinner!

Since you have boldness before God, my holy Guardian, pray to Him for my deliverance from the evils that harm me.

Holy Angel of the Lord, my Guardian, pray to God for me, a sinner!

Brightly illumine my soul, O bright Light, the Angel given to me by God, my instructor and guardian.

Glory to the Father, and to the Son, and to the Holy Spirit:

Though I sleep in the evil weight of sin, protect me as one who keeps vigil, O Angel of God, and rouse me to praise through your prayers.

Now and ever and unto ages of ages. Amen.

O Lady Mary, the unwedded Theotokos and hope of the faithful: Cast down the arrogance of the Enemy and give joy to those who hymn you.

ODE 6

Irmos: Beholding the Sea of Life raging with the storm of temptations, I have fled to Thy calm haven and cry to Thee: Deliver my life from destruction, O Most-merciful One!

Canon of Repentance

Have mercy on me, O God, have mercy on me!

I have lived my life on earth prodigally and committed my soul to darkness. Now, O Merciful Master, I pray: free me from the Enemy's labor and give me the intelligence to do Thy will.

Have mercy on me, O God, have mercy on me!

Who does what I do? As a pig wallows in mud, so do I serve sin! Pull me out of this mire, Lord, and give me the heart to accomplish Thy commandments.

Have mercy on me, O God, have mercy on me!

Lift yourself towards God, wretched man, recalling your transgressions! Fall down before the Creator with tears and groans! Being merciful, He will give you the mind to know His will.

Most Holy Theotokos, save us!

Keep us from both visible and invisible harm, O Virgin Theotokos! Receive my prayers, Most Pure One, and bear them to your Son, that He may give me the mind to do His will.

Canon to the Theotokos

Most Holy Theotokos, save us!

My nature was captive of death and corruption, O Virgin, but your Son and Lord saved it from both by surrendering Himself to death. Pray to Him for my deliverance from the evil deeds of my enemies.

Most Holy Theotokos, save us!

I know that you are the Intercessor of my life, O Virgin, my firm Protectress, healing the rebellions of temptations and dispelling the wiles of demons. I pray constantly that you will deliver me from my destructive passions.

Most Holy Theotokos, save us!

We have obtained you, O Maiden, as a wall of refuge and a most thorough salvation of souls. The multitude of human sorrows is not too great for you, and we ever rejoice in your illumination. Save us now, O Lady, from passions and misfortunes.

Most Holy Theotokos, save us!

I am lying on a bed of infirmity and there is no cure for my flesh. But I pray to you, the Good One who bore the God and Savior of the world: raise me from the destruction of illnesses.

Canon to the Guardian Angel

Holy Angel of the Lord, my Guardian, pray to God for me, a sinner!

I pray to you, holy Angel whom God has give to me as my good guardian: free me from every temptation!

Holy Angel of the Lord, my Guardian, pray to God for me, a sinner!

Shine light on my mind, O good one, and enlighten me! I pray you, holy Angel: teach me always to have wholesome thoughts.

Glory to the Father, and to the Son, and to the Holy Spirit:

Deliver my heart from this present noise, O my Guardian, and strengthen me to keep a good vigil, wondrously instructing me towards life-giving stillness.

Now and ever and unto ages of ages. Amen.

The Word of God dwelt in you, O Theotokos, and showed you to mankind as a Ladder to Heaven. Through you, He Who is on high came down to us.

Lord, have mercy! (Repeat three times.)

Glory to the Father, and to the Son, and to the Holy Spirit, now and ever unto ages of ages. Amen.

Kontakion, Tone 6

O my soul, why do you enrich yourself with sins? Why do you do the Devil's will? In what have you put your hope?

Cease all this and turn to God, weeping and crying: O compassionate Lord, have mercy on me, a sinner!

Ikos

Contemplate, my soul, the bitter hour of death and the dread judgment of your Creator and God. Threatening angels will seize you, my soul, and lead you to eternal flames. Repent before your death, therefore, crying: O Lord, have mercy on me, a sinner!

ODE 7

Irmos: The Angel made the furnace a source of dew for the pious youths, and the Will of God, which burned the Chaldeans, made the persecutor call out: Blessed art Thou, O God of our fathers!

Canon of Repentance

Have mercy on me, O God, have mercy on me!

Put not your hope in corruptible wealth, my soul, nor in things unjustly gathered. You do not know to whom you will leave it all. Instead, cry out: O Christ God, have mercy on me, the unworthy!

Have mercy on me, O God, have mercy on me!

Remember, my soul, both the eternal life and the Heavenly Kingdom prepared for the saints and the outer darkness and divine wrath prepared for the wicked. Then cry out: O Christ God, have mercy on me, the unworthy!

Have mercy on me, O God, have mercy on me!

Do not count on physical health, my soul, nor on fleeting beauty. You see how both the strong and the young die. Instead, cry out: O Christ God, have mercy on me, the unworthy!

Most Holy Theotokos, save us!

Fall down before the Mother of God, my soul, and pray to her, for she is the swift helper of penitents. She will entreat her Son, Christ God, and He will have mercy on me, the unworthy!

Canon to the Theotokos

Most Holy Theotokos, save us!

Desiring to establish our salvation, O Savior, Thou didst enter the Virgin's womb, showing her as the Intercessor for the world. Blessed art Thou, O God of our Fathers!

Most Holy Theotokos, save us!

Pray to Him Who is mercifully disposed and Whom you bore, O Pure Mother, that we may be delivered from transgressions and defilement of soul, who cry out with faith: Blessed art Thou, O God of our fathers!

Most Holy Theotokos, save us!

Thou didst show her who gave birth to Thee as a source of healing, a strong pillar, and a gate of repentance for those who cry out: Blessed art Thou, O God of our fathers!

Most Holy Theotokos, save us!

Grant healing from physical weakness and spiritual infirmities to those who draw near to your Protection with love, O Virgin Birthgiver of God, who bore Christ the Savior for us.

Canon to the Guardian Angel

Holy Angel of the Lord, my Guardian, pray to God for me, a sinner!

Have pity on me, Angel of the Lord, and pray to God for me, for He has given you to me forever as a helper, instructor, and guardian throughout my life.

Holy Angel of the Lord, my Guardian, pray to God for me, a sinner!

God entrusted my wretched soul to you undefiled, Holy Angel. Do not let it be killed by thieves on its journey, but direct it rather to the path of repentance.

Glory to the Father, and to the Son, and to the Holy Spirit:

I bring my soul, completely shamed by my evil thoughts and deeds. Hasten to me, my Instructor, and grant me the healing of good thoughts which lead me forever on the right path.

Now and ever and unto ages of ages. Amen.

For the sake of the Theotokos, O Personal Wisdom of the Most High, fill with wisdom and divine strength those who cry out: Blessed art Thou, O God of our fathers!

ODE 8

Irmos: Thou didst cause dew to pour from the flames over the pious youths, and didst burn the sacrifice of a righteous man with water—for Thou doest all things, O Christ, by Thy Will alone. We exalt Thee throughout all ages.

Canon of Repentance

Have mercy on me, O God, have mercy on me!

How can I not weep when I think of death? I have seen my brother lying in the tomb without glory and without form. What can I expect? What can I hope? Only grant me, Lord, repentance before the end. *(twice)*

Have mercy on me, O God, have mercy on me!

I believe that Thou wilt come to judge the living and the dead, and that everyone will stand in his rank: the old and the young; masters and princes; virgins and priests. Where will I find myself? Therefore, I cry out: grant me, Lord, repentance before the end.

Most Holy Theotokos, save us!

Receive my unworthy prayer, Most Pure Theotokos. Keep me from sudden death, and grant me repentance before the end.

Canon to the Theotokos

Most Holy Theotokos, save us!

O Virgin, do not disdain those who need your help, hymning and exalting you forever.

Most Holy Theotokos, save us!

You heal the infirmities of my soul and the illnesses of my body, O Virgin, that I may glorify you, O Pure One, forever.

Most Holy Theotokos, save us!

You pour an abundance of healing, O Virgin, on those who hymn you with faith and exalt your inexpressible birth-giving.

Most Holy Theotokos, save us!

You chase away the wiles of temptation and the onsets of passions, O Virgin. We therefore hymn you forever.

Canon to the Guardian Angel

Holy Angel of the Lord, my Guardian, pray to God for me, a sinner!

Most good Angel, sent from God: strengthen my life and never abandon me.

Holy Angel of the Lord, my Guardian, pray to God for me, a sinner!

I hymn you forever, most blessed and good Angel, the Instructor and Guardian of my soul.

We bless the Father, and the Son and the Holy Spirit, the Lord:

Be my protection and rampart on the day when all mankind will be tried and all deeds will be tested, both the good and the bad.

Now and ever and unto ages of ages. Amen.

Be the help and stillness of your servant, Ever-Virgin Theotokos, and never release me from your service.

ODE 9

Irmos: No man can see God, upon Whom the Angelic ranks dare not gaze. But through you, O Pure One, the Incarnate Word was revealed to mankind. Magnifying Him with the heavenly hosts, we call you blessed.

Canon of Repentance

Have mercy on me, O God, have mercy on me!

I now turn to you, angels, archangels, and all the heavenly host who stand by the throne of God: pray to your Creator that He deliver my soul from eternal torments.

Have mercy on me, O God, have mercy on me!

I now weep before you, holy patriarchs, kings and prophets, apostles and hierarchs, and all the elect of Christ: help me at the Judgment, that my soul be saved from the strength of the Enemy.

Have mercy on me, O God, have mercy on me!

I now lift up my hands to you, holy martyrs, desert-dwellers, virgins, righteous ones, and all saints who pray to the Lord for the whole world: may He have mercy on me at the hour of my death.

Most Holy Theotokos, save us!

Help me, Mother of God, for I have great hope in you! Pray to your Son, that when He sits to judge the living and the dead, He may place me at His right hand, even though I am unworthy.

Canon to the Theotokos

Most Holy Theotokos, save us!

O Virgin who bore Christ and wipes away every tear from every face: turn not away from my flowing tears.

Most Holy Theotokos, save us!

O Virgin who received the fullness of joy which destroyed the sorrow of sin: fill my heart with joy!

Most Holy Theotokos, save us!

Be a haven and intercession, an indestructible wall, a refuge, protection and rejoicing for those who run to you, O Virgin.

Most Holy Theotokos, save us!

Enlighten with the rays of your light those who in the True Faith confess you to be the Theotokos, O Virgin, dispelling the darkness of ignorance.

Most Holy Theotokos, save us!

Heal me, O Virgin, as I lie humbled on the place of misfortune, bringing me from illness to health.

Canon to the Guardian Angel

Lord Jesus Christ, my God, have mercy on me!

Have mercy on me, my only Savior, since Thou art merciful and compassionate, and join me to the choir of the Just

Holy Angel of the Lord, my Guardian, pray to God for me, a sinner!

Grant that I may always think and do what is good and useful, O Angel of the Lord, and show me to be strong and spotless in weakness.

Glory to the Father, and to the Son, and to the Holy Spirit:

Since you are bold before the Heavenly King, pray to Him with all the bodiless powers, that He may have mercy on me, a wretch.

Now and ever and unto ages of ages. Amen.

You have great boldness before the One Who took flesh from you, O Virgin. Remove me from my fetters and grant me freedom and salvation through your prayers.

CANON IN PREPARATION FOR HOLY COMMUNION

ODE 1 (Tone 2)

Irmos: Come, O people, let us sing a hymn to Christ God, Who divided the sea and guided the people Whom He led out of the bondage of Egypt, for He has glorified Himself.

Create in me a clean heart, O God, and put a new and right spirit within me.

May Thy Holy Body and Precious Blood, O Lord, be my Bread of everlasting life, healing me of various afflictions.

Cast me not away from Thy presence, and take not Thy Holy Spirit from me.

Make me worthy to partake of Thy most pure Body and Divine Blood, O Christ, for I am unworthy and accursed, defiled by unseemly deeds.

Glory to the Father, and to the Son, and to the Holy Spirit, now and ever and unto ages of ages. Amen.

You are the good soil, blessed Bride of God, which bore the ear of grain, the Savior of the world, which sprang from your untilled field. Grant that I may be saved by eating it.

ODE 3

Irmos: Having established me on the rock of faith, Thou hast strengthened me against my enemies. My spirit rejoices when I sing: There is none holy as our God, and none more righteous than Thou, O Lord!

Create in me a clean heart, O God, and put a new and right spirit within me.

Give me tears, O Christ, to cleanse the filth from my heart. Then, cleansed and with a good conscience, may I come with fear and faith to partake of Thy Divine Gifts, O Master.

Cast me not away from Thy presence, and take not Thy Holy Spirit from me.

O Lover of mankind, may Thy most pure Body and Divine Blood be for the remission of my sins, the communion of the Holy Spirit, life everlasting, and estrangement from passions and sorrows.

Glory to the Father, and to the Son, and to the Holy Spirit, now and ever and unto ages of ages. Amen.

Most holy Table of the Heavenly Bread which mercifully came down from on high, giving new life to the world; grant that I, who am unworthy, may now taste of Him in fear and live!

ODE 4

Irmos: Thou didst not come as an emissary or an angel, Lord, but from a Virgin, taking flesh and saving the fulness of my humanity. I therefore call out to Thee: Glory to Thy power, O Lord!

Create in me a clean heart, O God, and put a new and right spirit within me.

Because of human sins, Thou didst will to be slaughtered like a lamb, Most Merciful One Who wast incarnate for us. I pray, therefore: cleanse my sins as well.

Cast me not away from Thy presence, and take not Thy Holy Spirit from me.

Heal the wounds of my soul, Lord, and fully sanctify me. Grant, Master, that I, who am wretched, may partake of Thy Divine Mystical Supper.

Glory to the Father, and to the Son, and to the Holy Spirit, now and ever and unto ages of ages. Amen.

Incline towards me, O Lady, the One Who came from your womb. Keep me, your servant, undefiled and spotless, that I may be sanctified by receiving the spiritual pearl.

ODE 5

Irmos: Guide us in the light of Thy commandments, O Lord, the Giver of Light and Creator of the Universe. For we know no other God than Thee.

Create in me a clean heart, O God, and put a new and right spirit within me.

As Thou didst foretell, O Christ, so may it be with Thine inadequate servant, and abide in me according to Thy promise: for behold, I eat Thy Flesh and drink Thy Blood.

Cast me not away from Thy presence, and take not Thy Holy Spirit from me.

May the burning coal of Thy Body, O God and Word of God, be a light in my darkness, and may Thy Blood be the cleansing of my defiled soul.

Glory to the Father, and to the Son, and to the Holy Spirit, now and ever and unto ages of ages. Amen.

O Mary, Mother of God, precious Tabernacle of the divine Fragrance: make me a chosen vessel, by your prayers, that I may partake of the consecrated elements of your Son.

ODE 6

Irmos: Sunk in the depths of sin, I call on the unfathomable abyss of Thy compassion: Deliver me from destruction, O God!

Create in me a clean heart, O God, and put a new and right spirit within me.

Sanctify my mind, soul, heart, and body, O Savior! Grant, Master, that I may draw near, uncondemned, to the dread Mysteries.

Cast me not away from Thy presence, and take not Thy Holy Spirit from me.

By partaking of Thy Holy Mysteries, O Christ, may I be estranged from passions, joined to Thy Grace, and confirmed in life.

Glory to the Father, and to the Son, and to the Holy Spirit, now and ever and unto ages of ages. Amen.

Through the prayers of Thy holy Mother, O God, the Holy Word of God, sanctify me wholly as I come to Thy divine Mysteries.

Lord, have mercy! (Repeat three times.)

Glory to the Father and to the Son, and to the Holy Spirit, now and ever and unto ages of ages. Amen.

Kontakion, Tone 2:

Do not judge me unworthy to receive Thy Body and Divine Blood at this time. May the communion of Thy most pure and dread Mysteries not be to my condemnation, though I am wretched. Be it rather for eternal and everlasting life.

ODE 7

Irmos: The most wise youths would not serve the golden idol, but walked into the flames themselves, scorning the pagan gods. They sang amid the flames and an Angel bedewed them with the words: The prayer of your lips has been heard.

CANON IN PREPARATION FOR HOLY COMMUNION

Create in me a clean heart, O God, and put a new and right spirit within me.

May this communion of Thine immortal Mysteries, the fountain of good, O Christ, be my light, my life, and my dispassion. May it lead to progress and the increase of divine virtues, only Good One, that I may glorify Thee.

Cast me not away from Thy presence, and take not Thy Holy Spirit from me.

As I draw near to Thine immortal and divine Mysteries with love and trembling, may I be delivered from passions, enemies, want, and every sorrow. Grant that I may sing to Thee: blessed art Thou, Lord God of our fathers.

Glory to the Father, and to the Son, and to the Holy Spirit, now and ever and unto ages of ages. Amen.

To you who are full of the Grace of God and bore Christ the Savior beyond understanding, I your servant pray—the impure praying to the Pure One: cleanse me, who now wish to draw near to the most pure Mysteries, from all defilement of flesh and spirit.

ODE 8

Irmos: God came down upon the Hebrew youths in the fiery furnace and changed the flames into dew. Praise the acts of the Lord, and exalt Him throughout all ages!

Create in me a clean heart, O God, and put a new and right spirit within me.

O God, my Savior, allow me in my present despair to be a partaker of Thy heavenly, awesome, and holy Mysteries and of Thy divine and mystical supper, O Christ

Cast me not away from Thy presence, and take not Thy Holy Spirit from me.

Having run to Thy kindness, O Good One, I cry out to Thee in fear: be in me and I in Thee, as Thou didst say, O Savior! Behold: emboldened by Thy mercy, I eat Thy Flesh and drink Thy Blood.

Let us bless the Father, and the Son, and the Holy Spirit, the Lord; now and ever and unto ages of ages. Amen.

I tremble when I partake of fire, for fear that I might burn like wax or grass. O the awesome Mysteries! O the kind-heartedness of God! How can I, who am clay, commune of the Divine Body and Blood and become incorruptible?

ODE 9

Irmos: Our God and Lord, the Son of the Eternal Father, revealed Himself to us. He was incarnate of a Virgin that He might enlighten those in darkness and gather those who were scattered. We therefore magnify the all-hymned Theotokos.

Create in me a clean heart, O God, and put a new and right spirit within me.

Taste and see that this is Christ, the Lord Who of old became like us for us and Who, having once offered Himself as an offering to His Father, is forever immolated, sanctifying communicants.

Cast me not away from Thy presence, and take not Thy Holy Spirit from me.

May I be sanctified in soul and body, Master! May I be enlightened! May I be saved! May I become Thy dwelling through communion of the Sacred Mysteries, having Thee living in me with the Father and the Spirit, O Most Merciful Benefactor!

Glory to the Father, and to the Son, and to the Holy Spirit.

May Thy Body and Most Pure Blood, my Savior, be to me as fire and light. May they set flame to my sinful matter, burning the thorns of passions and fully enlightening me to worship Thy Divinity.

Now and ever and unto ages of ages. Amen.

God took flesh of your pure blood. Every race therefore hymns you, O Theotokos, and the intelligent multitudes glorify you, for through you we beheld the Ruler of all becoming substance in humanity.

PRAYERS IN PREPARATION FOR HOLY COMMUNION

Lord Jesus Christ, Son of God, through the prayers of Thy most pure Mother and all the saints, have mercy on us. Amen.

A priest uses the following:

Blessed is our God, always, now and ever, and unto ages of ages. Amen.

Glory to Thee, our God, glory to Thee.

O Heavenly King, the Comforter, the Spirit of Truth Who art everywhere and fillest all things. Treasury of Blessings and Giver of Life: Come and abide in us, and cleanse us from every impurity, and save our souls, O Good One.

Holy God! Holy Mighty! Holy Immortal! Have mercy on us. *(Repeat three times.)*

Glory to the Father, and to the Son, and to the Holy Spirit, now and ever and unto ages of ages. Amen.

O Most Holy Trinity, have mercy on us! Lord, cleanse us from our sins! Master, pardon our transgressions! Holy One, visit and heal our infirmities for Thy name's sake.

Lord, have mercy! *(Repeat three times.)*

Glory to the Father, and to the Son, and to the Holy Spirit, now and ever and unto ages of ages. Amen.

Our Father, Who art in heaven, hallowed be Thy Name. Thy Kingdom come. Thy will be done, on earth as it is in heaven. Give us this day our daily bread; and forgive us our trespasses, as we forgive those who trespass against us; and lead us not into temptation, but deliver us from evil.

If there is a priest, he adds the usual exclamation.

Lord, have mercy! *(Repeat twelve times.)*

Glory to the Father, and to the Son, and to the Holy Spirit, now and ever and unto ages of ages. Amen.

NOTE: When the Prayers in Preparation for Holy Communion are read immediately after Morning Prayers, we begin the former at this point.

Come, let us worship God our King!

Come, let us worship and fall down before Christ, our King and our God!

Come, let us worship and fall down before Christ Himself, our King and our God!

Psalm 22

The Lord is my shepherd, I shall not want;
> He makes me lie down in green pastures.

He leads me beside still waters;
> He restores my soul.

He leads me in paths of righteousness
> for His name's sake.

Even though I walk through the valley of the
> shadow of death
> I fear no evil;

for Thou art with me;
> Thy rod and Thy staff,
> they comfort me.

Thou preparest a Table before me
> in the presence of my enemies;

Thou anointest my head with oil,
> and most excellent is Thy Cup
> which brings me joy!

Surely goodness and mercy shall follow me

all the days of my life;
and I shall dwell in the house of the Lord
>for ever.

Psalm 23

The earth is the Lord's and the fulness thereof,
> the world and those who dwell therein;

for He has founded it upon the seas,
> and established it upon the rivers.

Who shall ascend the hill of the Lord?
> And who shall stand in His holy place?

He who has clean hands and a pure heart,
> who does not lift up his soul to what is false,
> and does not swear deceitfully.

He will receive blessing from the Lord,
> and vindication from the God of his
>> salvation.

Such is the generation of those who seek Him,
> who seek the face of the God of Jacob.

Lift up your heads, O gates!
> and be lifted up, O ancient doors!
> that the King of glory may come in.

Who is the King of glory?
> The Lord, strong and mighty,
> the Lord, mighty in battle!

Lift up your heads, O gates!
>> and be lifted up, O ancient doors!
>> that the King of glory may come in.
Who is this King of glory?
>> The Lord of hosts,
>> He is the King of glory!

Psalm 115

I kept my faith, even when I said,
>> "I am greatly afflicted";
I said in my consternation,
>> "Every man is a liar."
What shall I render to the Lord
>> for all His bounty to me?
I will lift up the Cup of Salvation
>> and call on the name of the Lord,
I will pay my vows to the Lord
>> in the presence of all His people.
Precious in the sight of the Lord
>> is the death of His saints.
O Lord, I am Thy servant;
>> I am Thy servant, the son of Thy handmaid.
>> Thou hast loosed my bonds.
I will offer to Thee the Sacrifice of Thanksgiving
>> and call on the name of the Lord.

I will pay my vows to the Lord
>in the presence of all His people,
in the courts of the house of the Lord,
>in your midst, O Jerusalem.

Glory to the Father, and to the Son, and to the Holy Spirit, now and ever, and unto ages of ages. Amen.

Alleluia! Alleluia! Alleluia! Glory to Thee, O God! *(Repeat three times.)*

And the following:

TROPARIA, TONE 8:

Disregard my iniquities, O Lord Who wast born of a Virgin! Cleanse my heart and make it a temple of Thy most pure Body and Blood. Turn me not away from Thy countenance, for Thy great mercy is immeasurable.

Glory to the Father, and to the Son, and to the Holy Spirit:

How dare I partake of Thy Holiness in my unworthiness? Even if I dare to approach Thee with the worthy, my garment accuses me, for it is not a wedding-garment, and I secure the condemnation of my most sinful soul. Cleanse, O Lord, the defilement of my soul and save me, for Thou lovest mankind.

Now and ever, and unto ages of ages. Amen.

Great is the multitude of my sins, O Theotokos! I come to you, O Pure One, in need of salvation. Visit my ailing soul, O You who alone are blessed, and pray to your Son and our God that He absolve the evil I have done.

NOTE: On Great and Holy Thursday, the following TROPARION is used, in TONE 8:

When the glorious disciples were enlightened at the washing of their feet before the supper, then the impious Judas was darkened, ailing with avarice, and to the lawless judges he betrayed Thee, the Righteous Judge. Behold, O lover of money, this man who because of money hanged himself. Flee from the greedy soul which dared such things against the Master. O Lord Who art good towards all men, glory to Thee!

If the Canon of Preparation for Holy Communion has not been read the preceding evening, it may be read here.

Lord, have mercy! *(Repeat forty times, with as many prostrations as desired.)*

Then, we read the following Verses of Instruction:

> When you intend, O man, to eat the Master's
> Body,

> Approach with fear, lest you be burned—for
> It is fire!
> Before drinking the Divine Blood in Communion,
> Make peace with those who have grieved
> you.
> Only then may you dare
> To eat the Mystical Food.

We also add the following verses:

> Before partaking of the Dread Sacrifice,
> The life-giving Body of the Master,
> Pray, trembling, in this manner:

1st Prayer, of Saint Basil the Great

O Lord and Master, Jesus Christ our God, the Fountain of life and immortality, the Creator of everything visible and invisible, the eternal and everlasting Son of the eternal Father: Thou hast come in these latter days because of the abundance of Thy goodness. Thou hast put on our human flesh and wast crucified and buried for us thankless and graceless men, and through Thine own blood Thou hast renewed our human nature which is corrupted by sin. And now, O Immortal King, accept the repentance of me a sinner, and incline Thine ear to me and listen to my words:

I have sinned, O Lord, I have sinned before heaven and before Thy face, and I am not worthy to look upon the height of Thy Glory.

I have provoked Thy goodness, I have transgressed Thy commandments, I have not obeyed Thy statutes.

But, O Lord, since Thou dost not remember evil, but art long-suffering and of great mercy, Thou hast not given me over to destruction for my lawlessness, but hast ever awaited my conversion.

O Lover of mankind, Thou hast said by Thy prophets: "I have no pleasure in the death of the wicked, but that the wicked turn from his way and live."

For Thou dost not wish, O Master, that the work of Thy hands should perish, neither dost Thou take pleasure in the destruction of men, but Thou desirest that all men should be saved and come to the knowledge of the truth.

Therefore, although I am unworthy both of heaven and of earth and of this passing life, having wholly yielded myself to sin and defiled Thine image, yet being Thy creature and of Thy making, I do not despair of my salvation in my wickedness. But made bold by Thine infinite compassion, I draw near.

Receive me, O Christ Who lovest mankind, as Thou didst receive the prostitute, the thief, the tax-collector and the prodigal. Take away the heavy burden of my sins, for Thou takest away the sins of the world, Thou healest the infirmities of mankind, Thou callest to Thyself and givest rest to those who labor and are heavy laden.

Thou hast not come to call the righteous, but sinners to repentance. Cleanse me from every stain of flesh and spirit. Teach me to fulfill holiness in fear of Thee, that having the testimony of my own conscience clean, and having communion of Thy holy things, I may be united with Thy Body and Blood and may have Thee to dwell and abide in me, with the Father and Thy Holy Spirit.

O Lord Jesus Christ my God, may the communion of Thy most pure and life-creating mysteries not bring me into judgment, nor may I become weak in soul and body by partaking in an unworthy manner, but grant me to receive communion of Thy holy things without condemnation even to my very last breath, and by them to receive communion of the Holy Spirit, provision for the journey of eternal life, and an acceptable answer at Thy dread judgment seat; that I, together with all Thy chosen ones, may also be a partaker of the incorruptible blessings which Thou hast prepared for those who love thee, O Lord, in whom Thou art glorified forever. Amen.

2nd Prayer, of Saint John Chrysostom

O Lord my God, I know that I am not worthy nor sufficiently pleasing that Thou shouldst come under the roof of the house of my soul for it is entirely desolate and fallen in ruin, and Thou wilt not find in me a place worthy to lay Thy head. But as Thou didst humble Thyself from on high for our sake, so now humble Thyself to my lowliness.

As Thou didst deign to lie in a cavern, in a manger of dumb beasts, so now deign to enter into the manger of my beastly soul, and into my soiled body.

As Thou didst not disdain to enter and to eat with sinners in the house of Simon the leper, so now be pleased to enter into the house of my soul, humble and leprous and sinful.

As Thou didst not cast away the sinful woman who came to touch Thee, so have compassion on me a sinner who comes to touch Thee.

As Thou didst not abhor the kiss of her sin-stained and unclean mouth, do not abhor my mouth, worse stained and more unclean than hers, nor my stained and shamed and unclean lips, nor my still more impure tongue.

But let the fiery coal of Thy most pure Body and Thy most precious Blood bring me sanctification, enlightenment and strengthening of my lowly soul and body, relief from the burden of my many transgressions, protection against every action of the devil, repulsion and victory over my wicked and evil habits, mortification of my passions, accomplishment of Thy commandments, increase of Thy divine grace, and inheritance of Thy Kingdom.

For I do not come to Thee in presumption, O Christ my God, but made bold by Thine inexpressible goodness, lest I stray far away from Thy flock, O Master, and become caught by the wolf of souls.

Therefore, I pray Thee, O Master, for Thou alone art holy: sanctify my soul and body, my mind and heart, my muscles and bones. Renew me entirely. Implant Thy fear in my fleshly members and let Thy sanctification never be removed from me.

Be my helper and defender, guide my life in peace and make me worthy to stand at Thy right hand with all Thy saints.

By the prayers and supplications of Thy most pure Mother, of Thy spiritual servants, the most pure angelic powers, and of all the saints who have been well-pleasing to Thee. Amen.

3rd Prayer, of Saint Simeon Metaphrastes

O only pure and incorruptible Lord! Because of the inexpressible mercy of Thy love for mankind, Thou didst take to Thyself our entire human composition from the pure blood of the Virgin who gave birth to Thee beyond nature, by the descent of the Holy Spirit and the good-will of the ever-existing Father.

O Christ Jesus, Wisdom of God and Peace and Power, through the human nature which Thou didst take to Thyself, Thou didst suffer the life-creating and saving passion: the Cross, the nails, the spear—death itself. Put to death in me the soul-destroying passions of the body.

Through Thy burial Thou didst capture the kingdom of death. Bury in me the evil devices of the devil with good thoughts, and destroy the spirits of evil.

Through Thy life-bringing Resurrection Thou didst raise up the first father who had fallen. Raise me up who am sunk down in sin and give me the image of repentance.

Through Thy glorious Ascension Thou didst deify the flesh which Thou didst assume, and placed it on the throne at the Father's right hand. Grant me to receive a place at the right hand with the saved through communion of Thy holy mysteries.

Through the coming of Thy Spirit, the Comforter, Thou didst make Thy consecrated disciples to be honorable vessels. Show me also to be the receptacle of His coming.

Thou hast promised to come again to judge the world in righteousness. Grant that I may go to meet Thee in the clouds, my Judge and Creator, with all Thy saints; that I may glorify and praise Thee without end, together with Thy Father Who is without beginning, and Thy most holy and good and life-creating Spirit, now and ever and unto ages of ages. Amen.

4th Prayer, of Saint John of Damascus

O Lord and Master Jesus Christ our God, Who alone hast power to absolve men from their sins, for Thou art good and lovest mankind: forgive all my transgressions done in knowledge or in ignorance, and make me worthy without condemnation to have communion of Thy divine and glorious and pure and life-creating mysteries. Let them not be for my punishment, or for the increase of my sins. But let them be for my purification and sanctification, as a promise of the life and Kingdom to come, a defense and a help and a repulsion of every attacker and the removal of my many transgressions. For Thou art a God of mercy and generosity and love for mankind, and to Thee we ascribe glory, with the Father and the Holy Spirit, now and ever and unto ages of ages. Amen.

5th Prayer, of Saint Basil the Great

I know, O Lord, that I have communion unworthily of Thy most pure Body and Thy most precious Blood, and that I am guilty and drink condemnation to myself not discerning Thy Body and Blood, O my Christ and God. But daring upon Thy generous loving-kindness I come to Thee Who hast said: "He who eats my flesh and drinks my blood abides in me and I in him." Be merciful, therefore, O Lord, and do not rebuke me, a sinner, but deal with me according to Thy mercy, and let Thy holy things be for my purification and healing, for enlightenment and protection, for the repulsion of every tempting thought and action of the devil which works spiritually in my fleshly members. Let them be for boldness and love for Thee, for the correction and grounding of my life, for the increase of virtue and perfection, for the fulfillment of Thy commandments, for the communion of the Holy Spirit, for the journey of eternal life, for a good and acceptable answer at Thy dread judgment, but not for judgment or condemnation. Amen.

6th Prayer, of Saint Simeon the New Theologian

From lips defiled
and a vile heart,
from an impure tongue
and a soul defiled,
receive my prayer, O my Christ,
and do not despise
my words, my appearance,
nor my shamelessness.
Grant me the boldness, my Christ,
to say what I desire
Even more—teach me
what to do and say.
I have sinned more than the harlot
who, on learning where Thou wast,
bought myrrh and came boldly
to anoint thy feet, my God,
my Master and my Christ
As Thou didst not turn her away
when she came with her heart,
so, O Word, turn me not away,
but give me Thy feet
to hold, to kiss,
and to anoint boldly
with a stream of tears
as a precious ointment.

Wash me with my tears, O Word,
and cleanse me with them!
Remit my transgressions
and grant me forgiveness.
Thou knowest the multitude of my evil:
Thou knowest also my wounds!
Thou seest my scars:
Thou knowest also my faith!
Thou seest my intentions
and hearest my sighs.
Nothing is hidden from Thee,
my God, my Maker, my Redeemer—
not even a tear-drop
or part of that drop.
Thine eyes have seen
that which I have not yet done.
Thou hast inscribed in Thy book
things yet to happen.
See my humility!
See each of my labors and all of my sins!
Absolve me, O God of all,
that with a pure heart,
trembling thoughts
and a contrite soul
I may partake of Thine undefiled
and most holy Mysteries

which enliven and deify
all who partake of them
with a pure heart.
Thou hast said, O Master:
"Whoever eats my Body
and drinks my Blood
abides in me
and I in him!"
True is every word
of my Master and God!
When I partake of Thy divine
and deifying Grace,
I am no longer alone—
I am with Thee, my Christ,
the Light of the Triple Sun
which enlightens the world.
May I not remain alone—
without Thee, O Life-Giver,
My Breath, my Life and my Joy,
the salvation of the world.
I approach Thee, therefore,
with tears, as Thou seest,
and a contrite soul.
I beg to receive
deliverance from my sins.
May I partake uncondemned

of Thy life-giving
and spotless Mysteries,
that Thou mayest abide,
as Thou hast said,
with me, the thrice-wretched.
May the Tempter not find me
without Thy Grace
and seize me deceitfully
and lead me, deceived,
from Thy deifying words.
Therefore, I fall down before Thee
and fervently cry:
as Thou didst receive the Prodigal
and the harlot who came to Thee,
O Gracious One, receive me,
prodigal and defiled.
With a contrite soul
I approach Thee now:
I know, O Savior, that no-one has sinned
against Thee as I have,
nor done the deeds
that I have done.
But I also know
that neither the greatness of my
transgressions
nor the multitude of my sins

surpass the great patience of my God
and His extreme love for mankind.
Through Thy merciful compassion
Thou dost cleanse and brighten
those who repent with fervor,
making them partakers of Light
and full communicants
of Thy Divinity.
To the astonishment of angels
and human minds,
Thou dost converse with them often
as with Thy true friends.
This makes me bold, my Christ,
this gives me wings!
Emboldened by the wealth
of Thy generosity towards us,
with both joy and trepidation,
I who am grass
partake of fire.
O strange wonder!
I am sprinkled with dew
and am not burned,
as the bush burned of old
without being consumed.
With grateful thoughts
and a grateful heart,

with my grateful members,
my soul and my body,
I now fall down and worship
and glorify Thee, my God,
for blessed art Thou,
now and for ever.

7th Prayer, of Saint John Chrysostom

O God, absolve, remit and pardon me my transgressions — as many sins as I have committed by word or action or thought, willingly or unwillingly, consciously or unconsciously; forgive me everything since Thou art good and lovest mankind. And by the prayers of Thy most pure Mother, of Thy spiritual servants, the holy angelic powers and all the saints, who from all ages have been well-pleasing to Thee, be pleased to allow me to receive Thy most pure Body and Thy most precious Blood for the healing of my soul and body, and the purification of my evil thoughts. For Thine is the Kingdom and the power and the glory with the Father and the Holy Spirit, now and ever and unto ages of ages. Amen.

8th Prayer, of Saint John Chrysostom

I am not worthy, Master and Lord, that Thou shouldst enter under the roof of my soul; yet inasmuch as Thou desirest to live in me as the Lover of mankind, I approach with boldness. Thou hast commanded: Let the doors be opened which Thou alone hast made and Thou shalt enter with Thy love for mankind just as Thou art. Thou shalt enter and enlighten my darkened reasoning. I believe that Thou wilt do this. For Thou didst not cast away the prostitute who came to Thee with tears, neither didst Thou turn away the tax-collector who repented, nor didst Thou reject the thief who acknowledged Thy Kingdom, nor didst Thou forsake the repentant persecutor, the Apostle Paul, even as he was. But all who came to Thee in repentance Thou didst unite to the ranks of Thy friends, Who alone art blessed forever, now and unto the endless ages. Amen.

9th Prayer, of Saint John Chrysostom

O Lord Jesus Christ my God, absolve, loose, cleanse and forgive me Thy sinful and useless and unworthy servant my errors, transgressions and sinful failing as many as I have committed from my youth up to this present day and hour, consciously and unconsciously, in words or actions or reasonings, thoughts, pursuits and in all my senses. By the prayers of Thy Mother the most pure and ever-virgin Mary who gave birth to Thee without human seed, my only hope which will not put me to shame, my intercessor and salvation, grant me to have communion without condemnation of Thy most pure, immortal, life-creating and awesome mysteries; for the remission of sins and unto life everlasting; for sanctification, enlightenment, strength, healing and health of soul and body; for the most perfect removal and destruction of my evil thoughts and reasonings and intentions, fantasies by night, brought by dark and evil spirits; for Thine is the Kingdom and the power and the glory and the honor and the worship with the Father and Thy Holy Spirit, now and ever and unto ages of ages. Amen.

10th Prayer, of Saint John of Damascus

I stand before the doors of Thy temple, and I do not forsake my wicked thoughts. But, O Christ my God, as Thou hast justified the tax-collector, and hast had mercy on the woman of Canaan and hast opened the gates of paradise to the thief, open to me the interior depths of Thy love for mankind and receive me as I come and repent before Thee. Receive me as Thou didst receive the sinful woman and the woman with the flow of blood. For the first embraced Thy most pure feet and received the forgiveness of her sins, and the second just touched the hem of Thy garment and received healing. But I who am lost, daring to receive Thy whole Body, may I not be burned; but receive me as Thou hast received them, and enlighten my spiritual senses, burning up my spiritual faults by the prayers of her who gave birth to Thee without human seed, and of the heavenly angelic powers, for Thou art blessed unto ages of ages. Amen.

Another Prayer of Saint John Chrysostom

I believe, O Lord, and I confess that Thou art truly the Christ, the Son of the living God Who camest into the world to save sinners, of whom I am first I believe also that this is truly Thine own most pure Body, and that this is truly Thine own precious Blood. Therefore, I pray Thee: have mercy upon me and forgive my transgressions both voluntary and involuntary, of word and of deed, committed in knowledge or in ignorance. And make me worthy to partake without condemnation of Thy most pure Mysteries, for the remission of my sins, and unto life everlasting. Amen.

As you approach to partake, say silently the following verses of Metaphrastes:

> Behold: I draw near to the Divine Communion.
> Burn me not as I partake, O Creator,
> For Thou art a Fire which burns the unworthy.
> Rather, cleanse me of all defilement.

Then say:

Of Thy Mystical Supper, O Son of God, accept me this day as a communicant; for I will not speak of Thy Mystery to Thine enemies, neither like Judas will I give Thee a kiss; but like the thief will I confess Thee: Remember me, O Lord, in Thy Kingdom.

And the following verses:

> Be awed, O man, when you see the deifying
> Blood!
> It is a fire which burns the unworthy!
> The Divine Body both deifies and nourishes me.
> It deifies the spirit and wondrously
> nourishes the mind.

Then, the following Troparia:

With love hast Thou drawn me, O Christ, and with Thy divine love hast Thou changed me. Burn away my sins with a spiritual fire and satisfy me with joy in Thee, that I may joyfully magnify Thy two comings, O Good One.

How shall I, who am unworthy, enter into the radiance of Thy saints? If I dare to enter the bridal-chamber, my garment accuses me, for it is not a wedding garment, and the angels will bind me and cast me out. Cleanse, O Lord, the filth of my soul and save me, for Thou lovest mankind.

And this prayer:

O Master Who lovest mankind! O Lord Jesus Christ my God! May these holy things not be to my condemnation, though I am unworthy of them. May they be for the cleansing and sanctification of my soul and body and a pledge of the life and Kingdom that are to come.

It is good for me to cleave to God and to place in the Lord the hope of my salvation

Then repeat:

Of Thy Mystical Supper, O Son of God, accept me this day as a communicant; for I will not speak of Thy Mystery to Thine enemies, neither like Judas will I give Thee a kiss; but like the thief will I confess Thee: remember me, O Lord, in Thy Kingdom.

PRAYERS OF THANKSGIVING AFTER COMMUNION

Glory to Thee, O God! Glory to Thee, O God! Glory to Thee, O God!

I thank Thee, O Lord my God, for Thou hast not rejected me, a sinner, but hast made me worthy to be a partaker of Thy holy things. I thank Thee, for Thou hast permitted me, the unworthy, to commune of Thy most pure and heavenly Gifts. But, O Master, Who lovest mankind, Who for our sakes didst die and rise again, and gavest us these awesome and life-creating Mysteries for the good and sanctification of our souls and bodies; let them be for the healing of soul and body, the repelling of every adversary, the illumining of the eyes of my heart, the peace of my spiritual powers, a faith unashamed, a love unfeigned, the fulfilling of wisdom, the observing of Thy commandments, the receiving of Thy Divine Grace, and the attaining of Thy Kingdom. Preserved by them in Thy holiness, may I always remember Thy Grace and live not for myself alone, but for Thee, our Master and Benefactor. May I pass from this life in the hope of eternal life, and so attain to the everlasting rest, where the voice of those who feast is unceasing, and the gladness of those who behold the goodness of Thy countenance is unending. For Thou art the true desire and the ineffable joy of those who love Thee, O Christ our God, and all creation sings of Thy praise forever. Amen.

A Prayer of Saint Basil the Great

O Master Christ our God, King of the Ages, Maker of all things: I thank Thee for all the good things Thou hast given me, especially for the communion with Thy most pure and life-creating Mysteries. I pray Thee, O gracious Lover of Man: preserve me under Thy protection, beneath the shadow of Thy wings. Enable me even to my last breath, to partake worthily and with a pure conscience of Thy holy things, for the remission of sins and unto life eternal. For Thou art the Bread of Life, the Fountain of Holiness, the Giver of all Good; to Thee we ascribe glory, with the Father and the Holy Spirit, now and ever and unto ages of ages. Amen.

A Prayer by Saint Simeon Metaphrastes

Freely Thou hast given me Thy Body for my food, O Thou Who art a fire consuming the unworthy. Consume me not, O my Creator, but instead enter into my members, my veins, my heart. Consume the thorns of my transgressions. Cleanse my soul and sanctify my reasonings. Make firm my knees and body. Illumine my five senses. Nail me to the fear of Thee. Always protect, guard, and keep me from soul-destroying words and deeds. Cleanse me, purify me, and adorn me. Give me understanding and illumination. Show me to be a temple of Thy One Spirit and not the home of many sins. May every evil thing, every carnal passion flee from me as from a fire as I become Thy tabernacle through communion. I offer Thee as intercessors all the saints: the leaders of the bodiless hosts, Thy Forerunner, the wise apostles, and Thy pure and blameless Mother. Accept their prayers in Thy love, O my Christ, and make me, Thy servant, a child of light. For Thou art the only Sanctification and Light of our souls, O Good One, and to Thee, our Master and God, we ascribe glory day by day.

Another Prayer

O Lord Jesus Christ our God: let Thy holy Body be my eternal life; Thy precious Blood, my remission of sins. Let this Eucharist be my joy, health, and gladness. Make me, a sinner, worthy to stand on the right hand of Thy glory at Thine awesome second Coming, through the prayers of Thy most pure Mother and of all the saints.

A Prayer to the Theotokos

O most holy Lady Theotokos, the light of my darkened soul, my hope, my protection, my refuge, my rest, and my joy: I thank you, for you have permitted me, the unworthy, to be a partaker of the most pure Body and precious Blood of your Son. Give the light of understanding to the eyes of my heart, you that gave birth to the True Light. Enliven me who am deadened by sin, you that gave birth to the Fountain of Immortality. Have mercy on me, O loving Mother of the merciful God. Grant me compunction and contrition of heart, humility in my thoughts, and a release from the slavery of my own reasonings. And enable me, even to my last breath, to receive the sanctification of the most pure Mysteries, for the healing of soul and body. Grant me tears of repentance and confession, that I may glorify you all the days of my life, for you are blessed and greatly glorified forever. Amen.

Lord, now lettest Thou Thy servant depart in peace, according to Thy word. For mine eyes have seen Thy salvation, which Thou hast prepared before the face of all people: a light to enlighten the Gentiles and to be the glory of Thy people, Israel.

Holy God! Holy Mighty! Holy Immortal! Have mercy on us. *(Repeat three times.)*

Glory to the Father, and to the Son, and to the Holy Spirit, now and ever and unto ages of ages. Amen.

O most-holy Trinity, have mercy on us! O Lord, cleanse us from our sins! O Master, pardon our transgressions! O Holy One, visit and heal our infirmities, for Thy name's sake.

Lord, have mercy! *(Repeat three times.)*

Glory to the Father, and to the Son, and to the Holy Spirit, now and ever and unto ages of ages. Amen.

Our Father, Who art in heaven, hallowed be Thy name, Thy Kingdom come. Thy will be done, on earth as it is in heaven. Give us this day our daily bread; and forgive us our trespasses, as we forgive those who trespass against us; and lead us not into temptation, but deliver us from evil.

If there is a priest, he adds the usual exclamation.

At the Liturgy of Saint John Chrysostom

Grace shining forth from your lips like a beacon has enlightened the universe. It has shown to the world the riches of poverty. It has revealed to us the heights of humility. Teaching us by your words, O Father John

Chrysostom, intercede before the Word, Christ our God, to save our souls.

Glory to the Father, and to the Son, and to the Holy Spirit:

You received Divine Grace from Heaven, all blessed and venerable John Chrysostom, and taught all by your mouth to worship one God in the Trinity. We praise you worthily, for you are an instructor who reveals things divine.

☦ ☦ ☦

At the Liturgy of Saint Basil the Great

Your proclamation has gone out into all the earth, for it was divinely taught by hearing your voice. You expounded the nature of creatures and ennobled the manners of men. O holy father of royal priesthood, entreat Christ God that our souls may be saved.

Glory to the Father, and to the Son, and to the Holy Spirit:

You were revealed as the sure foundation of the Church, granting all men a lord-ship which cannot be taken away, sealing it with your precepts, O venerable and heavenly father.

☦ ☦ ☦

At the Liturgy of the Presanctified Gifts Troparion of Saint Gregory the Dialogist

The truth of things revealed you to your flock as a rule of faith, an Icon of meekness, and a teacher of abstinence. You thus reached the heights through humility and wealth through poverty. O holy hierarch, father Gregory, pray to Christ God for the salvation of our souls.

☦ ☦ ☦

Now and ever and unto ages of ages. Amen.

Steadfast protectress of Christians, constant advocate before the Creator: do not despise the cry of us sinners, but in your goodness come speedily to help us who call on you in faith. Hasten to hear our petition and to intercede for us, O Theotokos, for you always protect those who honor you.

Lord, have mercy! (Repeat twelve times.)

Glory to the Father, and to the Son, and to the Holy Spirit, now and ever and unto ages of ages. Amen.

More honorable than the Cherubim, and more glorious beyond compare than the Seraphim: without defilement you gave birth to God the Word. True Theotokos, we magnify you.

The priest pronounces the dismissal.

INDEX

altar, 13, 40
Angel, 2, 21, 68, 73, 75, 82, 83, 85, 86, 90, 93, 94, 96, 97, 98, 100, 101, 104, 107, 114
anger, 21, 66, 72, 73, 75
Apostle Paul, 140
Apostles, 22, 50, 71
Apostolic, 14, 25, 30, 45
Archangels, 22
Biblical scholars, 7
Blessings, 8, 36, 119
Blood, 25, 109, 110, 112, 114, 116, 117, 118, 124, 126, 128, 130, 133, 136, 139, 142, 143, 147, 148
bloodguiltiness, 12, 39
Bride of God, 18, 59, 84, 89, 93, 110
burden, 28, 128, 130
Canon, 46, 80, 81, 82, 83, 84, 85, 87, 89, 90, 91, 92, 93, 94, 95, 96, 98, 99, 100, 102, 103, 104, 105, 106, 107, 125

Cherubim, 23, 32, 35, 46, 57, 74, 152
commandments, 10, 18, 44, 57, 60, 61, 78, 82, 83, 95, 112, 127, 130, 133, 145
communion with God, 5
Cross, 22, 49, 54, 55, 65, 68, 77, 131
crucified, 13, 14, 45, 126
Departed, 30
deserts, 28
Divine Liturgy, 5, 6
divine Spirit, 18
Dread Sacrifice, 126
Elders of Optina, 23
Eucharist, 147
Fathers, 49, 50, 71, 99
fountain of life, 43
Gehenna, 91
Heaven, 13, 25, 37, 70, 97, 150
Heavenly Table, 35
hieromonks, 28
history of the Church, 5
Holy Mountain, 28
Holy Scriptures, 7

Holy Spirit, 8, 9, 10, 11, 12, 13, 14, 16, 23, 26, 32, 33, 34, 35, 36, 37, 39, 42, 44, 45, 46, 47, 48, 51, 52, 57, 61, 62, 63, 64, 65, 68, 72, 74, 75, 76, 82, 86, 90, 93, 97, 101, 104, 107, 109, 110, 111, 112, 113, 114, 115, 116, 117, 119, 120, 124, 128, 131, 133, 139, 141, 146, 149, 150, 152

Holy Trinity, 9, 10, 32, 37, 46, 62, 73, 74, 120

holy Virgin, 19

holy Will, 23

human life, 21

Hymn, 46, 86

Ikos, 98

illumined heart, 15

Immortal King, 16, 67, 126

Irmos, 46, 79, 83, 87, 91, 94, 98, 101, 105, 109, 110, 111, 112, 113, 114, 116, 117

Israel, 79, 148

Jacob, 122

Jerusalem, 13, 39, 124

Jesus Christ, 8, 13, 16, 20, 23, 25, 36, 42, 43, 45, 58, 60, 62, 65, 68, 70, 71, 73, 75, 77, 82, 107, 119, 126, 128, 132, 140, 144, 147

Judge, 10, 16, 125, 132

Kingdom, 9, 14, 15, 33, 34, 37, 45, 47, 52, 63, 64, 70, 88, 99, 120, 130, 132, 139, 140, 141, 143, 144, 145, 149

Kontakion, 56, 74, 87, 97, 114

laborers, 27

Last Day, 87

Light, 13, 16, 18, 31, 35, 45, 65, 91, 93, 112, 136, 138, 147, 148

Litany, 61

Martyrs, 22, 48, 51, 71

mercy, 8, 9, 10, 11, 23, 26, 27, 28, 29, 30, 31, 32, 33, 34, 35, 36, 37, 38, 43, 44, 46, 47, 48, 49, 53, 54, 55, 56, 57, 58, 60, 61, 62, 63, 64,

65, 68, 70, 72, 73, 74,
75, 76, 78, 80, 82, 83,
84, 86, 87, 88, 91, 92,
94, 95, 97, 98, 99,
102, 105, 106, 107,
108, 鯥 114, 116, 119,
120, 121, 124, 125,
127, 131, 133, 141,
142, 148, 149, 151
Midnight Song, 18
monastery, 5, 26, 27
Monk Antiochus, 60
Monk Paul, 59
mortal body, 21
Mother of God, 72, 74,
76, 80, 81, 89, 92, 99,
106, 113
Mysteries, 46, 113, 114,
115, 116, 117, 135,
137, 142, 145, 146,
148
Mystical Food, 126
Nourisher, 35
ODE, 79, 83, 87, 91, 94,
98, 101, 105, 109,
110, 111, 112, 113,
114, 116, 117
orphans, 29
Orthodox Christians, 5,
7, 22, 29, 31, 49, 78

Orthodox Church in
America, 6
Orthodox liturgical
Psalter, 6
Patriarchs, 26, 30
Patron Saint, 22
Pharaoh, 79
Pontius Pilate, 13, 45
priest, 9, 27, 36, 37, 47,
58, 63, 119, 120, 149,
152
Prodigal, 92, 137
Prophets, 22
Providence, 30
Psalm, 11, 38, 40, 41, 79,
121, 122, 123
Repentance, 80, 83, 87,
91, 94, 98, 102, 105
Rule of Prayer, 5
Russian Church, 4, 46
sacrifices, 13, 40
Saint Basil the Great,
126, 146, 150
Saint John Chrysostom,
149
Saint Simeon
Metaphrastes, 146
Saints, 4, 22, 71, 73, 77,
78

salvation, 12, 13, 21, 25, 29, 30, 39, 40, 45, 50, 51, 54, 57, 60, 64, 65, 67, 77, 81, 90, 96, 99, 108, 122, 125, 127, 136, 140, 144, 148, 151

Septuagint, 7

Seraphim, 23, 32, 35, 46, 57, 75, 152

servant, 15, 16, 19, 21, 25, 41, 42, 58, 65, 67, 70, 73, 82, 83, 104, 112, 115, 123, 140, 147, 148

Sign of the Cross, 8, 77

Simon the leper, 129

sinfulness, 10

soul, 4, 18, 19, 21, 22, 23, 41, 42, 43, 60, 64, 65, 67, 70, 71, 72, 73, 74, 75, 76, 81, 83, 84, 85, 86, 87, 88, 91, 92, 93, 94, 97, 98, 99, 100, 101, 103, 104, 105, 111, 112, 113, 117, 121, 122, 124, 125, 128, 129, 130, 131, 134, 135, 136, 137, 139, 141, 143, 鯳 144, 145, 147, 148

spiritual fragrance, 25

St. Antiochus, 65

St. Basil, 16, 17, 57, 133

St. Ephraim, 58, 59

St. Ioannikios, 74

St. John Chrysostom, 69, 129, 139, 140, 142

St. John of Damascus, 75, 132, 141

St. Macarius, 14, 15, 16, 64, 67

St. Simeon Metaphrastes, 131

St. Simeon the New Theologian, 134

statutes, 44, 127

Studite monk, 72

Theotokos, 4, 9, 10, 18, 21, 22, 23, 32, 35, 46, 48, 51, 56, 57, 59, 60, 64, 68, 72, 73, 74, 76, 77, 78, 80, 81, 84, 85, 87, 88, 89, 92, 93, 94, 95, 96, 97, 99, 100, 101, 102, 103, 104, 106, 107, 117, 118, 125, 148, 151, 152

Throne of God, 5

INDEX

Tone, 46, 52, 53, 54, 55, 56, 63, 79, 86, 87, 97, 109, 114
torments, 19, 60, 69, 75, 105
troparia, 6
Verses of Instruction, 125
vigil, 94, 97
widows, 29
Word, 20, 23, 32, 35, 46, 54, 57, 59, 65, 75, 81, 91, 97, 105, 112, 114, 134, 135, 150, 152
worship, 11, 19, 37, 38, 42, 44, 54, 60, 66, 118, 120, 121, 139, 141, 150

www.ingramcontent.com/pod-product-compliance
Lightning Source LLC
Chambersburg PA
CBHW060610080526
44585CB00013B/762